THEN and NOW

Discovering my Viennese Family

Irving M. Adler
With Frances L. Adler

Front Cover Photo:
Photography by John Gevers Photography; photo composition by Amy Keller.

DEDICATION

This book is dedicated to my mother, the grandmother
I never met and all the relatives I never knew.

*March 1932 photo of my
grandmother, Clara, with her
daughter and my mother, Elsa.*

We Remember Them

This poem by Rabbis Sylvan Kamens and Jack Riemer* best describes my feelings about the Viennese family that I grew up with in New York City and the Viennese family that I only know about through the letters my mother received and kept.

In the rising of the sun and in its going down, we remember them.

In the blowing of the wind and in the chill of winter, we remember them.

In the opening of buds and in the rebirth of spring, we remember them.

In the blueness of the sky and in the warmth of summer, we remember them.

In the rustling of leaves and in the beauty of autumn, we remember them.

In the beginning of the year and when it ends, we remember them.

When we are weary and in need of strength, we remember them.

When we are lost and sick at heart, we remember them.

When we have joys we yearn to share, we remember them

So long as we live, they too shall live, for they are now a part of us,

as we remember them.

Table of Contents

Preface

On May 3, 2018, my cousin, Shaul Spielmann, spoke words of dedication for a Stone of Remembrance for his parents, Benno and Josefine Spielmann, who were victims of the Holocaust. He was standing in the courtyard of the apartment building at Fleischmarkt 22, in the first district of Vienna. It was their last home in Vienna before they were deported to the camps.

Shaul, surrounded by his family and friends from Israel, the U.S. and Vienna, spoke movingly about the horrors he and his parents had endured.

In 1938, when he was 7 years old, Nazi thugs broke into his apartment at Klausgasse 33 in the 16th district, put a gun to his head, and threatened his parents with their son's death unless they gave up all their valuables. Then, a few months later, they were relocated to the building at Fleischmarkt 22.

In 1942, the family was deported to Theresienstadt and then to Auschwitz-Birkenau, where Shaul's mother, Josefine, was murdered. His father, Benno, was sent to Buchenwald, where he was murdered. In January 1945, Shaul was on a death march from Auschwitz. Eventually he arrived at the Mauthausen sub-camp at Melk. In April 1945, he was marched to the Mauthausen sub-camp at Gunskirchen. He survived and was finally liberated in May 1945. After he regained his health, he emigrated to Israel – at age 14, and all alone in the world. Today he lives in Ashkelon with his wife, Miriam. Their beautiful family includes seven children, 18 grandchildren and 4 great-grandchildren.

In May 2014, I had dedicated a Stone of Remembrance for my grandmother, Clara Bader Nichtern. A few years earlier I had discovered letters that my grandmother wrote from 1938 to 1941 to her daughter Elsa, my mother, before my grandmother was killed in the Holocaust. Those letters led to my learning about relatives I hadn't known and my journey to find them. Events directly tied to this May 2014 Stone of Remembrance dedication led to the discovery and meeting with my cousin Shaul, who was by then the only remaining member of my family who had survived the Holocaust.

In his words on that day at Fleischmarkt 22, Shaul recounted his tragic experience. His words ended with "today, with very deep sorrow, I finally close a circle."

THEN and NOW is the story about the relatives I never knew, especially my grandmother; who they were; their daily experiences, as described in my grandmother's letters, as they lived through Nazi occupation; and what happened to them. *THEN and NOW* is the story about what I learned along the way, eventually leading me to find Shaul and to close my circle.

Prologue: Who Are These People?

INTRODUCTION

After returning from an August 2010 trip to Vienna with my wife, Fran, I discovered 102 letters from my grandmother and other relatives to my mother, who had escaped from Vienna to England and then to the United States in the leadup to the Holocaust.

The letters covered the period from September 1938 until November 1941. Most of the letters were from a mother to a daughter, two people with an incredibly strong bond. Since they were so close emotionally, the letters from my grandmother were written as a stream of consciousness – as if they were sitting directly opposite each other and there was no distance between them, instead of 900 miles from September 1938 to February 1940 and 4,200 miles from March 1940 to November 1941.

As the letters were being transcribed and translated, I discovered names of family members and family friends who were completely unknown to me. Although surprising at first, this was not a total shock, since my mother hardly ever spoke about her life in Vienna, the Nazi occupation after the *Anschluss*[1], and any relatives and friends who were victims of the Holocaust, including her mother.

The breakthrough in the writing of this book occurred in July 2017, when Fran and I visited Dr. Elizabeth "Betsy" Anthony (currently Director of Visiting Scholar Programs at the United States Holocaust Memorial Museum's Mandel Center for Advanced Holocaust Studies) in Washington, D.C., and spent two days discussing the letters with her. Betsy found the key! She pointed out that the letters told the story of family members and close family friends, many of whom became victims of the Holocaust, and also described many of the tragic events affecting the whole Jewish population of Vienna under Nazi occupation: from the first letter, written on September 20, 1938, to the last letter, dated November 17, 1941.

---

[1]   *Anschluss* refers to the annexation of Austria in 1938. The German Army marched into Austria on March 12, 1938. On March 13, 1938, Austria was incorporated into the Greater German Reich. Source: www.theholocaust-explained.org.

This book also traces the journey that, in July 2014, led me to the discovery of and meeting with the only member of my family who lived through the Holocaust and is still alive today, my cousin Shaul. He was totally unaware that any member of his Viennese family was still alive.

This multi-year research project included visiting the sites where my relatives lived; examining original documents and databases in the archives of the Jewish Community of Vienna, the archives of the City of Vienna and the International Tracing Service (now Arolsen Archives); researching several Holocaust victims databases, especially those of the Center for the Documentation of the Austrian Resistance and Yad Vashem; analyzing both English and German scholarly works on the Holocaust in Vienna; and dedicating Stones of Remembrance for relatives who were victims of the Holocaust. It was a chance meeting at one such dedication ceremony that broke through the brick wall of who had survived and eventually led me to find the last family member who had lived through the Holocaust and was still alive.

Firsthand accounts of the Holocaust are becoming fewer each day with the passing of the last remaining survivors. As the child of survivors and the grandson of a Holocaust victim, I hope to use this book, **THEN *and* NOW**, as a way to shed some light on the lives of the Jews of Vienna and of my Viennese relatives so that future generations of my family, as well as others who read this, can get some understanding of what life was like in the struggle to survive under Nazi occupation.

THE DISCOVERY

Growing Up

Irv with his parents in 1948

I was born in 1943 and spent most of my first nine years with my family and extended family on the upper west side of New York City, which – based on what I understand today – was sort of a Vienna transplanted. I am not sure when I first heard the word Holocaust – probably sometime in the late-1970s/early-1980s. As I got older, I realized that I had European parents. And then I realized that they were Viennese. And then I realized that everyone in my family had come from Vienna – but I had no clue what that meant.

When I was 9 years old and my younger brother, Ron, was 2, my parents moved the family to Far Rockaway, where I grew up. I went to Brooklyn Technical High School and then to New York University. After receiving my undergraduate degree from New York University in 1965, I went to the University of Michigan for graduate school, and I have lived in the Midwest ever since.

I grew up knowing my father's parents – who lived in the same building and helped raise me – and my mother's father, Theodore Nichtern, and his wife Olga, who I later learned was his third wife. I didn't know my maternal grandmother. Some of my family history started to unfold while I was in high school and continued while I was in college and graduate school. I found out later that my father had been imprisoned in the Dachau and Buchenwald concentration camps, that one of my uncles had had a factory in Vienna that was taken over by the Nazis ("Aryanized"), and that my father was able to get his parents out of Vienna and eventually into the United States, by way of Italy and Portugal, because of some work he had done for Westinghouse in support of the war effort.

I don't recall exactly when, but I found out later that my maternal grandmother had not gotten out of Europe and had been killed by the Nazis. I had no idea how and where she'd died; and whenever I tried to talk with my mother about this, the conversation was very short, as my mother would become very emotionally distraught and was unable to talk about anything.

As I was growing up, I got bits and pieces of the story at various times, but no one ever sat down with me to tell me what had happened in Vienna or the details of why the people I knew and met growing up were in the U.S. I would occasionally meet other Viennese family members. I knew they had left Vienna to escape the Nazi persecution; but as with everything else, I had no details and certainly no understanding of what that really meant. And I knew virtually nothing about the family members who did not get out. Basically, it was a closed subject. No one really wanted to relive the past and to talk about it. End of story!

My Parents' Move to Florida

My mother and father moved to Fort Lauderdale, Florida, in 1974. Periodically, I would make family visits, and we would have some brief talks about family history. Over the ensuing years, I got to know some of my family's history, probably more about my father's side of the family, as there were fewer of them and they were all in the U.S. I also learned a little more about my maternal grandfather's side of the family, many of whom (the ones who had made it to the U.S.) I met as I was growing up in New York, as well as my mother's uncle, aunt and cousin, who lived in Detroit – but virtually nothing about my maternal grandmother's side of the family.

In 1985, I took my family to Austria for a vacation. We spent time in Vienna. We even went to the apartment house where my mother and her mother had lived, at Hütteldorfer Straße 117. The trip and the visit to where my mother and her mother had once lived was very meaningful, but it didn't have the impact on me that it does today.

In 1996, my father passed away. My mother and I decided it was time for her to move from her condo to a nearby independent-living facility. During this move I started to go through the various pieces of paper and files that my parents had accumulated over the years, and I came across a leather-bound suitcase that could have been a prop from the set of the movie *Casablanca*. It had originally belonged to my Uncle Hans, the uncle who had owned the factory in Vienna. It contained various papers relating to my American-Viennese family: photo albums, burial-plot papers, citizenship papers, Austrian pension receipts, and pre-1945 materials – passports, birth certificates, school records, my father's 1939 release papers from Buchenwald – and a small, tight bundle of papers in an old and yellowed plastic pouch, approximately 5 x 7 inches, with a zipper on top. That suitcase was what remained of my family's historical archives.

In 1998, during a visit to my mother at the independent-living facility, I sat down with her and told her that we needed to go through the suitcase. We sat down and pulled out some old photo albums. I finally got her to provide some more details on her mother and other family members. For once she seemed very cooperative and willing to talk, so we went through the pictures of family members, many of whom I didn't know or had never even heard of. I did know some family members, especially the Nichterns, as I had met them while I was growing up in New York City. Once I left for Ann Arbor and the University of Michigan, I lost most of my connections to them except for my mother's uncle, Julius Nichtern, who lived in Detroit. When I went home to New York, I rarely saw other relatives; and by that time my maternal grandfather, Theodore Nichtern, had passed away and I had lost touch with Olga's family.

I don't know why my mother was more willing to talk about her past in Vienna on that one occasion, but she was. I took some notes; and, for the first time, I pieced together a very rudimentary family tree and put names to faces, to the limited extent that I could.

My mother also showed me photos of her mother and of relatives and friends on my grandmother's side of the family. She provided some first names but no last names, as she struggled to match them with faces. My mother also mentioned some letters from her mother and pointed out the package of letters she had saved, but that was all. She also showed me some family documents related to her father that she had kept, as well as documents related to my father's side of the family.

I didn't realize it at the time, but my mother, who was 87, was starting to lose her mental faculties. Shortly thereafter, she had a stroke. She required several months of rehabilitation and lost most of her ability to speak. The stroke also marked the onset of dementia, which, over the next five years, continued to get worse as she moved from the rehabilitation facility to assisted living and then finally to nursing homes, all in the general area of Fort Lauderdale, where she spent the last three years of her life barely saying another word.

Since my mother couldn't take many personal possessions with her over the course of these moves, I took the suitcase back to Fort Wayne with me. I periodically opened it to look at various documents, especially those that related to her status as an Austrian pensioner, but not much else.

My mother passed away in December 2003. The conversation that I had with her in 1998 turned out to be the last one we ever had about her mother and that side of my family – and it hadn't provided a lot of information.

Shortly after my mother's funeral, I took a more detailed look at the suitcase. I focused on various records associated with her birth, her schooling, and her

Austrian pension. Other than picking up the plastic bag containing the letters and putting it back into the suitcase, I did nothing else with the letters or with the suitcase other than transferring some of the important papers to a safe deposit box. I took the suitcase with the letters, the photo albums and some of the papers and put it in the back of a closet – where it remained for most of the next seven years. I opened it occasionally to look for some family information, such as the New York City burial-plot information of family members, birth records and some school records, but I never looked at the packet of letters.

August 2010 – A Vienna Vacation?

In late July 2010, my wife, Fran, and I took a vacation to Europe, which included stops in Prague, Budapest and Vienna, the last stop in the trip. We got to Vienna late in the afternoon of Sunday, August 8. It was a bright and sunny day, so we decided to take a walk and wanted to see the Holocaust memorial at *Judenplatz*, designed by British artist Rachel Whiteread. This is the area in the inner city where Jews were allowed to settle in medieval times.

The Memorial at Judenplatz

After we had spent some time looking at the memorial, we noticed a small museum in a corner of the plaza, on the site of an excavated medieval synagogue. We entered and looked around. In the museum shop, I saw a woman sitting behind a counter that held pamphlets about the Viennese Jewish community. I struck up a conversation with the woman and told her that my Viennese grandmother had been killed during the Holocaust and asked her where I could get more information about Holocaust victims. She said that we should go to the Center for the Documentation of Austrian Resistance *(Dokumentationsarchiv des Österreichischen Widerstandes, or the DÖW)*[2] and told us how to get there. After leaving the museum, Fran and I wandered around looking for the

---

2   Documentation Center of Austrian Resistance *(Dokumentationsarchiv des Österreichischen Widerstandes)* commonly known as the DÖW. The Documentation Center of Austrian Resistance chronicles and explores the actions of those individuals and organizations that practiced resistance in Austria during the Nazi dictatorship of World War II. The Center was founded by a group of former members of the Austrian resistance, victims of Nazi persecution, and scholars. The main intention is to preserve important remnants of the history of the time and inform current and future generations about Nazi crimes. The Center performs extensive work and activities related to the subject, including conducting research, performing archival work on previously existing and new material as it becomes available, creating educational materials for schools and publications, saving oral histories, and maintaining informational databases. One such database is "Registration by Name: Austrian Victims of the Holocaust." Source: Documentation Centre of Austrian Resistance in Vienna - Travelers411.

location of the DÖW among the narrow winding streets and small alleyways of the *Innere Stadt* (inner city). We found the entrance to the DÖW and decided that we would try to go there the next day to see what we could find out.

We arrived shortly after 9 a.m., rang the bell, and were asked to come up to the first floor, where we were greeted by an elderly woman. We told her that we had no appointment, but that the woman at the *Judenplatz* museum had suggested that we come here. After we'd waited a few minutes, the elderly woman who had greeted us escorted us into an office where we first met Dr. Elisabeth Klamper, a DÖW archivist. After about 15 minutes of searching through records on her computer, Dr. Klamper raised her head from behind the computer screen, her face ashen. "I have some very bad news to tell you," she said. "Your grandmother was killed at Maly Trostinec." I had no idea what she was talking about. I had never heard of Maly Trostinec.

Dr. Klamper gave us a brief overview of the Maly Trostinec extermination camp[3]. It was located on the southeastern edge of Minsk, Belarus, about 12 km from the center of Minsk. About 10,000 Viennese Jews were among the approximately 200,000 men, women and children murdered at Maly Trostinec, including my grandmother, who was deported from Vienna on June 9, 1942. Dr. Klamper also told us that my grandmother had been moved to a different address within the city before her deportation. The Nazis murdered her at Maly Trostinec on June 15, 1942.

After we met with Dr. Klamper, what had been planned as a five-day vacation resulted in two and a half days of researching records at the offices of the Jewish Community of Vienna *(Israelitische Kultusgemeinde*, commonly referred to as the IKG)[4] and the Archives of the City of Vienna to find out everything we could about my family, especially on my mother's side. It was at the IKG where I saw the original Jewish community records of my mother's birth. All the records were in large, leather-bound ledgers, written in a beautiful ornate script that, for the most part, was illegible to me. It was at the City Archives that we noticed that my grandmother's name had disappeared from the 1941 "Lehmann" Vienna city directory. We didn't know what that meant.

---

3   The Nazi concentration camp Maly Trostinec became the largest Nazi concentration camp in the territories of the former Soviet Union. Between spring 1942 and summer 1944, between 60,000 and 200,000 people were murdered at the camp, according to different estimates. Jews from Western Europe were the largest group among the victims, with an estimated 22,000 German Jews among them, according to the Dortmund-based International Education and Exchange Center (IBB).Source: www.dw.com/en/belarus-an-unknown-story-of-the-holocaust-brings-forgotten-camp-back-into-europes-conscience.

4   The *Israelitische Kultusgemeinde* (IKG), the Jewish Community of Vienna, was founded in 1852. It regulated all aspects of Jewish life throughout Vienna: synagogues, finances, schools and education, and philanthropic activities. The offices of the IKG were housed in the building complex associated with the *Stadttempel* (city temple) on Seitenstettengasse in the inner city. In March 1938, the offices of the IKG were ransacked. In November 1938, as Jewish buildings were ravaged and destroyed, only the *Stadttempel* survived. The IKG was disbanded in 1942 and replaced by the Council of Elders, the *Ältestenrat*. The IKG was re-established after World War II.

We headed home after five days in Vienna, knowing more than we knew when we started, but still lacking any in-depth knowledge of my grandmother's side of my family.

The Letters

When we got back home, I started to think about how and where I could get more information on my grandmother and my mother's life in Vienna. I can't say for sure when it happened, but I had an epiphany: Maybe there was something in the suitcase that could shed some light on this.

As I was rummaging through the suitcase, I rediscovered the plastic pouch with the letters. I took it out and removed the bundle, about the size of a 4 x 6-inch pack of index cards, held together by a faded pink ribbon. Untying that packet of letters, I started to realize that it might not have been touched for 60 years or more. I untied the ribbon and started to remove the letters from the tightly wound bundle, one by one and very carefully. Some were damaged, but most were in good shape. Some were on conventional writing paper. Some were on very thin tissue paper. Others were about the size of a standard piece of copy paper. Still others were about twice that size. Most had multiple authors and were completely covered with writing.

There were 102 letters in all, written from 1938 to 1941, including one letter, written by my mother in November 1941, that was returned to her in July 1942.

The letters through May 1940 were written in a very ornate cursive style, in which I could hardly distinguish individual letters, let alone words. I found out later that these letters were written in the old-style cursive called *Kurrentschrift*. The letters from June 1940 through November 1941 were written in a more modern style of cursive known as *Lateinschrift*. I was able to make out the dates and it appeared that the letters were addressed to my mother, except for the last letter from my mother.

Looking back at this discovery, I realized that I didn't quite know what I had. But I did know enough to grasp that the letters might represent a diary of my grandmother's life under Nazi occupation. I knew immediately that I needed to get the letters translated so that I could read them and learn about the grandmother I never knew.

It took several years, but by 2014 all the letters had been translated so I could read what was in them. Later all the letters were transcribed; and because I had worked to resurrect my German translation skills, I was able to read them, as well as other scholarly works, to better understand what Vienna was like following the *Anschluss*.

This marked the beginning of my journey to understand the content and meaning of the decades-old correspondence between my grandmother and other relatives with my mother, initially covering the 900 miles between Vienna and London and then covering the 4,200 miles between Vienna and New York City.

WHAT HAPPENED IN AUSTRIA?

But before I discuss the letters in more detail, I would like to give an overview of the events in Austria that led up to the letters.

Conditions in Post-*Anschluss* Vienna

Map of Annexation of Austria by Nazi Germany Source:
www.historyonthenet/nazi-germany-Anschluss.com

On March 12, 1938, Nazi troops marched into Austria and took over the country. This takeover, known as the *Anschluss*, was the defining event in the contemporary history of Austria and its people, especially its Jews. Within 48 hours, Austria was relegated to a province and incorporated into "Greater Germany." Austria was now the Ostmark – the new eastern edge of the Reich.

The lives of Austrian Jews, more than 90% of whom lived in Vienna, became a nightmare. During the following days, it started to become clear that the history, the culture and the life that the Jews had known in Vienna for multiple generations was gone forever. Before the *Anschluss*, there were about 201,000 Jews living in Austria, about 186,000 of them in Vienna. After the *Anschluss*, most Jews living outside Vienna were moved into Vienna. During the next seven years about 130,000 fled; about 66,000 died or were murdered; and by the war's end, only about 5,000 remained.[5]

Austrian anti-Semitism had been building up during the course of the previous decades. It exploded during the days and weeks immediately after the *Anschluss*. The Nazis' so-called racial anti-Semitism found fertile ground in Vienna, with its age-old religiously motivated anti-Judaism.

During the first six weeks after the *Anschluss*, the Jews of Vienna experienced all at once what the Jews of Germany had experienced in five years of progressively increasing Nazi persecution. The anti-Jewish legislation that had been put in place in Germany starting in 1933, including the Nuremberg racial laws of

---

5   Based on data developed by the historian Jonny Moser and given in *Demographie der jüdischen Bevölkerung Österreiches 1938-1945*, Dokumentationsarchiv des österreichischen Widerstandes, Vienna, (1999).

1935, was implemented in Austria within weeks of the *Anschluss*; and on May 20, 1938, it became law. Using the analogy of the frog in the pot of hot water, the German Jews in 1933 were like the frog who was put into lukewarm water, and the temperature of the water increased steadily over the next five years until it was boiling. Right after the *Anschluss*, the Austrian Jews were like the frog who was plunged immediately into boiling water.

Still, this was only the beginning: Over the next months and years, the Jews of Austria faced ever-tightening restrictions of their freedoms. (See Appendix A for anti-Jewish regulations.)

In the weeks after Austria's incorporation into Greater Germany, hundreds of Viennese Jews committed suicide. During those first weeks, Nazi thugs, many of them Viennese, beat and murdered Jews on the street, desecrated synagogues, robbed and looted department stores, invaded apartments occupied by Jews, and confiscated their belongings.

On March 16, 1938, Adolf Eichmann[6] arrived in Vienna and took over the IKG, which was then raided by the *Gestapo*[7] on March 18, 1938. The *Gestapo* shut down the IKG, and its administration was jailed. The IKG was reopened on May 2, 1938, under the control of Eichmann, with its main goal being the emigration of the Viennese Jewish population. (The IKG continued to function until November 1942, when it was disbanded and replaced by the *Ältestenrat*, the Council of Elders of the Jewish Community of Vienna. The IKG was reestablished once again after World War II.)

On March 26, 1938, Hermann Göring, commander-in-chief of the *Luftwaffe* (the German air force) and Plenipotentiary of the Four-Year Plan, stated during a speech in front of a wildly cheering audience at Vienna's Northwest Railway Station that he would rid Vienna of its Jews within four years.

Immediately after the *Anschluss*, the illegal "wild Aryanization" of Jewish businesses took place, in which Jewish owners were forcefully expelled from their establishments. By the end of April, through pseudo-legal means, the Nazi authorities established the property registration office. At the same time that

---

6   Adolf Eichmann (1906-1962) headed *Gestapo* Department IV B4 for Jewish Affairs, serving as a self-proclaimed Jewish specialist. He played a crucial role in the practical execution of a plan to murder Jews - "the Final Solution of the Jewish Question." With the Nazi takeover of Austria in March of 1938, Eichmann was sent to Vienna where he established a Central Office for Jewish Emigration. This office had the sole authority to issue permits to Jews desperately wanting to leave Austria and became engaged in extorting wealth in return for safe passage. About 130,000 Austrian Jews managed to leave, with most turning over all their worldly possessions to Eichmann's office. The process developed by Eichmann and his associates was known as the "Vienna Model" and was duplicated in other cities where significant Jewish deportations occurred such as Prague and Berlin. Sources: Adolf Eichmann - Biography (historyplace.com) and Adolf Eichmann - a central figure in the implementation of the Final Solution | www.yadvashem.org

7   The *Gestapo* (Geheime Staatspolizei) was the German state police during the Nazi regime.

the Nazis were taking over Jewish businesses, they were also expelling Jews from their homes and apartments, throwing them out into the streets, to relieve a decades-old Viennese housing shortage. Non-Jews, especially those with ties to Viennese Nazis, then moved into the homes of the evicted Jews, who had to move in with other family members or friends or into group apartments. These group apartments became the foundation for the "collection apartments" later used to stage Jews for their deportation to the camps.

In April, many prominent Viennese individuals, including many leaders of the Jewish community, were arrested and sent to the German concentration camp Dachau, outside of Munich. Then in late May/early June, a mass arrest of Jewish men occurred: About 2,000 Jewish men were arrested on the streets, in cafes and in their homes, held without charge at a collection site in the 20th District, at Karajangasse, and then taken to Dachau.

It was during this March-May 1938 timeframe that Austrian Nazis and their Viennese sympathizers focused their abuse and humiliation on the Jews and implemented actions to remove the Jewish community from the economic life of Vienna. The objective at that time was to force the Jewish population to leave the country.

Eichmann allowed the IKG to reopen on May 2, 1938, with the goal of removing the Jews from Vienna as quickly as possible through forced emigration. Jewish communal organizations provided up-to-date information on the various immigration policies operating throughout the world in journals such as *Jüdische Auswanderung* (Jewish Emigration), which was published in Berlin through 1939.[8] In Vienna, the IKG published the *Zionistische Rundschau* (Jewish News Circular).[9]

This was the environment that my mother and my grandmother were living in during those first weeks and months after the *Anschluss*.

Shortly after the reopening of the IKG and the establishment of the IKG's Emigration Department, the heads of Jewish households filed emigration questionnaires covering about 40,000 Viennese Jews, a number that grew to almost 118,000 Viennese Jews by October.

---

8   *Jüdische Auswanderung* was a journal about emigration and settlement published in Berlin from 1936 to 1939 by Verlag Schmoller & Gordon. Source: Jüdische Auswanderung : Korrespondenzblatt über Auswanderungs- und Siedlungswesen in SearchWorks catalog (stanford.edu).
9   The *Zionistische Rundschau*, controlled by Adolf Eichmann, was published from May 20 to November 9, 1938. The paper was focused on providing information that would help Jews leave the Reich, such as information on emigration, advertisements for ship companies, foreign language lessons, retraining courses and information about foreign countries as emigration locations. From Offenberger, L.F., *The Jews of Nazi Vienna, 1938-1945*, Palgrave McMillian, Cham, Switzerland, (2017) p. 81.

This is the emigration questionnaire that my grandmother filled out for herself and her daughter.

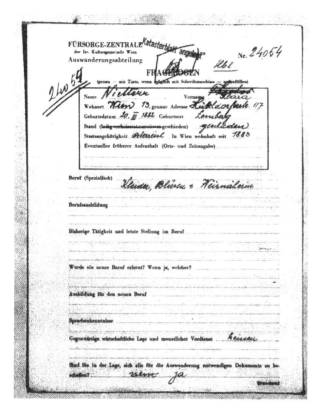

Page 1 of Clara's IKG Emigration Questionnaire

(Source: IKG-Vienna)

Translation:
Welfare Head Office of the Jewish Community of Vienna
Emigration Department   Number:
Questionnaire
(Last)Name: First Name:
Place of residence: Exact Address:
Date of Birth: Place of Birth:
Marital Status (single, married, widowed, divorced):
Nationality: Vienna residence since:
Earlier stay (Place & Date):
Profession (Specialty):
Professional Education:
Previous work and last job in this profession: Was a new profession learned? If so, which?
Training for the new profession:
Knowledge of a foreign language:
Present economic condition and monthly income:
Are you in the position to get all necessary documents for emigration?

Page 2 of Clara's IKG Emigration Questionnaire

(Source: IKG-Vienna)

Translation:

To where do you want to emigrate?

What plans do you have for your new residence?

What (economic) resources are available to you for the emigration?

What connections do you have in the foreign country, especially in the country to where you want to emigrate?

	First & Last Name	Residence	Exact Address	Degree of Relationship
Relatives				
Friends				

References:

Do you have a valid passport? Issued by:

Dependent Family Members

Degree of Relationship	Name	Place of Birth	Birth Date	Profession

Which of the above-named family members shall emigrate now and which later?

Vienna on .... 193...   Signature

Nr. 3, 3. Juni 1938   ZIONISTISCHE RUNDSCHAU   Seite 3

Die jüdische Wanderung

Die Tätigkeit der Kultusgemeinde:

Planmäßige Emigration

Die Auswanderungsabteilung der Israelitischen Kultusgemeinde gibt folgendes bekannt:

1. Mit der Durchführung der planmäßigen jüdischen Emigration aus Deutschösterreich sind von der zuständigen Behörde beauftragt worden:

a) Für Wanderung nach allen Ländern mit Ausnahme Palästinas die Auswanderungs-Abteilung der Israelitischen Kultusgemeinde Wien, I. Seitenstettengasse 2–4.

b) Für die Auswanderung nach Palästina: Das Palästinaamt in Wien, I. Marc Aurelstr. 5.

2. Zur Erfassung aller auswanderungsbereiten Juden ist die Ausfüllung des von der Auswanderungs-Abteilung der Kultusgemeinde ausgegebenen Fragebogens notwendig. Diese Fragebogen sind unentgeltlich im Hause Wien I. Seitenstettengasse 4, Parterre, erhältlich, woselbst auch die ausgefüllten Bogen abzugeben sind.

3. Die Behandlung der bereits über 25.000 eingereichten Fragebogen kann naturgemäß nur allmählich erfolgen. Gegenwärtig hat eine persönliche Vorsprache im Amte nur für solche Parteien Zweck, die bereits eine Einreisebewilligung in irgend ein Land besitzen. In diesem Falle sind alle erforderlichen Dokumente und Nachweise mitzubringen. Parteienverkehr bei dieser Sektion der Auswanderungsabteilung täglich von 9–1 Uhr.

4. Auswanderungsmöglichkeiten in europäische Länder sind derzeit im allgemeinen nicht gegeben, in Betracht kommen in der Regel nur Stellen für Hausgehilfinnen, welche für England, Holland und Schweden durch die besondere Beratungsstelle vermittelt werden. (Parteienverkehr Montag und Donnerstag von 2–6 Uhr nachm. im Hause I. Seitenstettengasse 4, 2. Stock.)

8. Vor einer Auswanderung ins Altreich oder unnötigen Reisen dorthin wird nachdrücklichst gewarnt.

9. Die Auswanderungsabteilung steht auch zur Erteilung von Ratschlägen in Bezug auf die Durchführung der Reisen selbst wie Besorgung der Schiffs- und Bahnkarten, Beförderung von Gepäck, etc. den Auswanderern zur Verfügung.

10. Zwecks Durchführung einer planmäßigen Emigration sowie im Interesse der Auswanderer selbst wird vor einer übereilten Liquidierung von Vermögenschaften, beziehungsweise Geschäften dringendst gewarnt. Die Auswanderer sollten erst dann allfällige, nicht mitzunehmende Vermögensteile veräußern, sobald es endgültig feststeht, daß sie in absehbarer Zeit auswandern können. Welche Bestimmungen hinsichtlich einer Überführung von Geld oder Waren ins Ausreichland in Anwendung kommen werden, wird erst nach Erlassung der bezüglichen gesetzlichen Anordnungen bekannt sein.

An alle Auswanderer!

Alle Auswanderer werden gebeten, vor ihrer Abreise bei der Israelitischen Kultusgemeinde Wien Meldung über ihre Auswanderung zu erstatten, gleichgültig, ob zu dieser die Hilfe der Kultusgemeinde in Anspruch genommen wurde oder nicht.

Alle in Wien wohnhaften Juden werden darauf aufmerksam gemacht, daß die einzige von den Behörden zugelassene jüdische Zeitung Österreichs die „Zionistische Rundschau" ist. Alle Kundmachungen und Veröffentlichungen jüdischer Stellen werden nur in dieser Zeitung erscheinen. Alle Wünsche und Anfragen, Pläne und Vorschläge sind, insofern es sich um die Auswanderung nach Palästina handelt, ...

Ärzteberatung

Im Rahmen der Auswanderungsaktion der israelitischen Kultusgemeinde eingerichtete Beratungsstelle für Ärzte, welche Montag und Donnerstag zwischen 6 und 8 Uhr. ... Es wird ersucht, diese Beratung nur in ganz dringenden Fällen mit präziser Fragestellung aufzusuchen. ...

Umschichtungskurse

Zwecks beruflicher Ausbildung erwachsener Auswanderer durch Umschichtungskurse in den Berufen des Handwerks, der Landwirtschaft und der Hauswirtschaft werden hiermit

a) fachlich und pädagogisch ausgebildete Lehrer,

b) Handwerksmeister (mit und ohne Werkstätten)

c) Landwirte, Gärtner, Geflügelzüchter,

d) Hauswirtschafterinnen und Inhaberinnen von Kochschulen

e) Inhaberinnen von Nähschulen (Kleider- und Wäschemacherei Modisturei, u.s.w.)

ersucht, sich an die Fürsorgezentrale der israel. Kultusgemeinde Wien, I. Seitenstettengasse 2 (Berufsausbildungs- und Umschichtungsstelle),

4. The emigration opportunities to European countries are currently not generally available. As a rule, under consideration are only positions for housemaids for England, Holland and Sweden which will be arranged through special counseling centers. (Open on Monday and Thursday from 2 to 6 PM at house at 1 Seitenstettengasse 4, 2nd floor)

June 3, 1938 Issue of "Zionistische Rundschau"

On June 3, 1938, the Jewish community in Vienna informed readers on Page 3 of the *Zionistische Rundschau*, about the possibility of a domestic permit for England.

This was the series of events that motivated my mother, Elsa, to apply for a visa at the U.S. Consulate in Vienna on May 10, 1938; to have my grandmother, Clara, submit an emigration questionnaire to the IKG on May 23, 1938, for herself and for her daughter; for my mother to seek employment as a domestic worker in Great Britain; and then on September 12, 1938 – Elsa's 27th birthday – to pack up and depart Vienna by train from the *Westbahnhof* (Western Railway Station), and never see her mother again.

Escape to England as a Domestic

During the First World War, well over 1 million women went to work in British industry in support of the war effort, while the British men were sent to Europe to fight the war.

After the end of the war, these women had to be integrated back into the peacetime economy.

During the war many English households had reduced their use of domestic servants. Now they wanted to return to their earlier way of life, creating a demand for household help. However, British women were reluctant to return to domestic service, since their World War I work experience had changed their outlook about becoming maids again. This reluctance led to a shortage of domestic service workers in England during the interwar years and to the opening of opportunities for female foreign workers who could get jobs as domestics with the aid of the domestic permit. The permit was issued on condition that no British citizen could be found for the vacancy. With domestic permits, maids and other domestic workers could enter the United Kingdom (UK) without a lot of bureaucratic hassle. Many Austrian women took this opportunity and applied for positions in England.

During the 1930s, an infrastructure was developed to hire and bring women to England to work as domestics. Organizations in Vienna, such as the *Englisch-Österreichische Damen und Dienerschaftsunion* (The English-Austrian Ladies and Servants Union) worked together with English employment agencies to send young Austrian women as maids to English private households.

Before the *Anschluss*, the percentage of Jewish girls who applied for domestic permits was very low because they were reluctant to become servants when other alternatives such as white-collar or factory jobs in their home countries were available. After the Nazis took over Germany and then Austria, they introduced a program to induce non-Jewish German and Austrian maids to return to their countries of origin. This exodus of workers significantly increased the need for household help in the UK.

From the *Anschluss* through 1939, the opportunity to get a job in England as a domestic offered about 10,000 Austrian Jewish women, 45 or younger like my mother, an escape pathway from Vienna. The *Englisch-Österreichische Damen und Dienerschaftsunion* was the employment agency through which my mother got her job as a domestic in England. Below is an example of the advertisement that this employment agency ran in the Viennese papers. Could this have been the one that my mother saw that led to her employment in England as a domestic?

Die Neue Freie Presse, *June 26, 1938, page 34*

Translation:
Open Positions Female

Translation:
England
Cooks and Parlor Maids with references obtain jobs through Öst-Engl. D. and D. Union.
7 Wimbergergasse13 98823-5m

Elsa's IKG Training Notebook

Säuglinge und Kinder *Infants and Children*
Pflege und Pädagogik *Care and Pedagogy*

Once my mother decided that her escape from Vienna was through the English domestic-servant program, she enrolled in an IKG training course for domestic servants so that she would have the knowledge and skills to succeed. I confirmed this when I discovered her domestic training book consisting of 60 pages of hand-written class notes. Here is the front cover and a page from her IKG domestic-training notebook, which contained information on how to care for babies and children as well as other information on cooking and cleaning needed by English domestics.

Translation:

Small child 1-2 years
Morning: 200 grams whole milk, Malzkaffee
Cocoa, Ovaltine, Zwieback
Broken up cookies.
Eating time: Bowl of milk (or bread and butter with fruit) preferred.
Lunch: (possibly soup) Vegetable, compote (possibly dessert) Snack break: Same as morning.
Dinner: Semolina or vegetables.
The child must eat well.
At 16 months old, soft sausage, minced veal, not much meat until 2 years old.
With [....] cook with vegetable fat
Spoon measurements
Teaspoon 5 grams.
Baby spoon 10 grams.
Tablespoon 15 grams.

Page from Elsa's IKG Training Notebook

Supported by the IKG training classes and knowing that the British domestic-servant program was an escape route from Nazi-occupied Vienna, my mother, as well as other relatives and friends in Vienna, took advantage of this path to freedom. From September 16, 1938, until February 16, 1940, my mother lived in England. During that time, she had two different employers: The first was a Mrs. Turle at Avril, Highmoor Road, Sherborne, Dorset. The second was the wife of Reverend Claude Rutledge Cotton, the vicar of the St. Mary's church at Ladywell Road in Lewisham, S.E. 13.

I remember my mother talking a little about her second job and saying how the vicar loved her cooking. My mother never commented about her first job. It is highly likely that working as a domestic servant saved my mother's life. (See Appendix B for Elsa's domestic permit.)

Women like my mother and other relatives became refugees in a foreign country and endured many difficulties associated with life in Britain before and during the war years; but most importantly, they were able to escape from Vienna and to survive. Some told their story; and some, like my mother, did not.

NAMES

The packet of letters that I found in 2010 contained mostly complete letters. There also were some fragments of letters and a few notes. After identifying the fragments and examining the notes, I have assembled, identified and dated 102 letters. (See Appendix C.) One hundred and one of these letters were written by my grandmother and by other relatives. The letters begin 6 months after the *Anschluss* and 1½ months before *Kristallnacht*[10]. They cover the period from September 20, 1938, until November 30, 1941. The last letter in the collection, dated November 30, 1941, was written by my mother to my grandmother. It never reached my grandmother and was returned to my mother in July 1942. It is the only letter I have that was written by my mother.

As I was reading these letters, I came across names of people whom I had never heard of before. In total, there were close to 250 names of relatives, friends, acquaintances and other persons mentioned in the letters, including people who lived at the Hütteldorfer Straße 117 apartment building. (See Appendix D for apartment building dwellers and Appendix E for list of names identified in the letters.) Talking about these people was my grandmother's way of conveying the daily events in her life as well as those around her as she communicated with my mother, at first from hundreds and then later from thousands of miles away.

In my reading and re-reading of the letters, it became clear that in addition to my grandmother, Clara, whose name I found out during the conversation that I had with my mother in 1998, and my Aunt Mali, whose name came up when my mother, typically under emotional stress, told me that she got her Aunt Mali out of Vienna instead of her mother, there were persons that were frequently mentioned in the letters. Who were they?

Over a period of several years, I have researched the names of the persons who appeared most frequently in the letters. As I was doing this, it became clear that most of these names were tied together. They appeared to be family members or people who were very close to my grandmother and were a part of her extended family and daily life.

---

10   *Kristallnacht*, the Night of Broken Glass, also called the November Pogrom, was a pogrom against Jews carried out by Nazi paramilitary forces and civilians throughout Nazi Germany on November 9-10, 1938. The German authorities looked on without intervening. The name *Kristallnacht* comes from the shards of broken glass that littered the streets after the windows of Jewish-owned stores, buildings and synagogues were smashed. Rioters destroyed 267 synagogues throughout Germany, Austria and the Sudetenland. Over 7,000 Jewish businesses were damaged or destroyed, and 30,000 Jewish men were arrested and incarcerated in concentration camps. In Vienna, the *Stadttempel* was the only Jewish building that survived the destructive rampage. Source: Kristallnacht - Wikipedia.

Here are the names of the persons who appeared frequently in the letters. I have tried to identify them and provide information about their relationship to one another. These are the people who, at various levels, were participants in this sad story.

- Clara Nichtern (born Bader). My grandmother.

- Elsa Adler (born Nichtern). My mother.

- Leon (Leo), Amalia (Mali) (born Mihaly) and Markus (Maxl) Bader. Leo was my mother's uncle and the brother of Clara Nichtern. Mali was my mother's aunt (by marriage). Their son, Maxl, was the youngest of my mother's four first cousins on the Bader family side.

- Anna Spitz and her children, Carl, Otto and Greta. My grandmother's first cousin on the Bader family side. Referred to in the letters as Tante Spitz.

- David and Max Sokal. The brothers of Anna Spitz and Clara's first cousins.

- Theodore Nichtern. My grandfather. Only husband of Clara Nichtern. Married three times. Referred to as Father. His third wife, Olga, accompanied him to America.

- Henrietta (Henny) Spitzer. My mother's stepsister. Olga's daughter by her second marriage.

- Fritz Kaltenbrunner. My mother's apparently very serious boyfriend.

- Israel and Rosalie Spielmann (born Bader and my grandmother's sister). Referred to as Uncle Spielmann and Tante Sali.

- Benno, Josefine (Pepi) and Paul (sweet little Pauli). Benno Spielmann was the oldest of the three Spielmann siblings who were my mother's first cousins on the Bader family side.

- Max Spielmann was second oldest of the three Spielmann siblings who were my mother's first cousins on the Bader family side.

- Emma, Adolf (Dolfi) and Kurt (Kurtl) Löff. Emma (born Spielmann) was the youngest of the three Spielmann siblings who were my mother's first cousins on the Bader family side.

- Siegfried, Erna and Edith Löff. Siegfried and Erna were the brother and sister-in-law of Dolfi Löff. Their daughter, Edith, was on the first *Kindertransport*[11] from Vienna to London.

---

11   The *Kindertransport* (German for "children's transport") was an organized rescue effort that took place during the nine months before the outbreak of the Second World War. The United Kingdom took in nearly 10,000 predominantly Jewish children from Nazi Germany, Austria, Czechoslovakia and Poland, and the Free City of Danzig. The children were placed in British foster homes, hostels, schools and farms. Often, they were the only members of their families who survived the Holocaust. Source: *Kindertransport* - Wikipedia.

- Egon Weiss was the first cousin of Adolf and Siegfried Löff. He was able to obtain affidavits[12] for the Löff families.

- Anna and Julius Singer. My mother's aunt and uncle. Anna was the sister of Theodore Nichtern. Referred to as Tante Singer and Uncle Julius. They had two sons, Siegfried (Fritz) and Adolf (Dolfi), who were in England, and a daughter, Eva, who was with them in Vienna. They were my mother's first cousins on the Nichtern family side.

- Ernestine and Felix (Selig) Atlas and their children, Herta, Gertrude (Trude) and Edith (Titta). They were very close family friends of my grandmother. Felix's brother, Philip Atlas, had been married to Clara's sister Yetti, who died in 1918.

- Joseph Bernhard Nichtern. My mother's uncle and the brother of Theodore Nichtern. Referred to as Uncle Bernhard.

- Salamon (Rolf) Nichtern. My mother's uncle and the youngest brother of Theodore Nichtern.

- Julius, Millie and Edith Nichtern. My mother's uncle, and the brother of Theodore, aunt and one of my mother's Nichtern-side first cousins.

- Karl Nuechtern. My mother's uncle and brother of Theodore. Was the first Nichtern sibling to go to America.

- Jakob Altenberg. Extremely close family friend of the Singers. Took over the role as provider of monthly living allowance to Clara in 1940, once Uncle Bernhard was incapacitated.

- Fritz's mother. No name given. However, address of Fritz's mother given in my mother's address book. Based on this, I believe that her name was Antonia Kaltenbrunner. As far as I know, she was not related to that infamous Austrian Nazi, Ernst Kaltenbrunner.

- Hanni Tant. Fritz's aunt and married sister of Antonia Kaltenbrunner.

- Helene Diamand. Best friend of my grandmother. They had known each other since childhood.

- Michel Salter. A very close friend of my grandmother.

---

12   The affidavit signed by a sponsor was a commitment to provide financial support to an immigrant so that that immigrant is not a financial burden to the admitting state, in this case the U.S. Source: uscis.gov.

- Members of the Mihaly family: Fanny (the mother), Adolf (Dolfi), Margarete (Gretl) Beck (born Mihaly), Helene (Helli), Ernestine (Tini) and Gertrude (Gerti/Trude and daughter of Margarete). These were the mother, siblings and niece of Amalia (Mali) Bader.

- Pauline Markstein, second wife of Theodore, and her children Richard and Gertrude (Trude) Markstein.

- British employers: Mrs. Turle, Mrs. Cotter and the Lux family.

  Now on to their story.

Part I: Then - "Even If I Could See You Just One More Time"

If my grandmother, Clara Bader Nichtern, had lived, she would have been only 61 when I was born and would probably have been a significant figure in my life. But she was murdered in the Holocaust, at the infamous extermination site of Maly Trostinec. I didn't have the opportunity to know her and really knew very little about her. In fact, I don't think I knew her name until my mother said it during our 1998 conversation. Everything I know about her life I have learned from the 102 letters that I discovered.

The letters have the feel of an ongoing conversation. In many cases, it was easy to visualize Clara and Elsa sitting across from one another at the kitchen table having a cup of tea and chatting about the events of the day. And although I have only one side of this correspondence, Clara responds so specifically to things Elsa has written that it's almost as if we have Elsa's side of the conversation, too.

The narrative built from the letters tries to bring to life the story of my grandmother and her relatives and friends, during four years in Vienna under Nazi occupation. (See Appendix F for dates of important events during this time period.) It is encapsulated in the tragic theme that permeates all the letters, "Even if I could see you just one more time." It is said many times and in many ways between mother and daughter and between other relatives. But for many, this was never meant to be!

VIENNA: 1938-1941

1938 – "Don't worry! Everything is calm"

Elsa left Vienna on September 12, 1938 – her 27th birthday and exactly six months after the *Anschluss*, Germany's takeover of Austria. She arrived in England on September 16 after a stop in Belgium, including a visit with her cousin, Otto Spitz. Less than two weeks later, on September 29, Great Britain, France, Italy and Germany signed the Munich Agreement.[13] And on the next day, Jewish doctors in Austria lost their right to practice medicine.

Clara and Elsa were exceptionally close. It had been just the two of them together for 17 years since Clara and her husband, Theodore, had divorced; so it was especially gut-wrenching for Elsa to leave her mother and for Clara to be alone in the apartment at Hütteldorfer Straße 117.

Clara was very anxious about Elsa after her move and concerned that she hadn't heard from her, so she was very relieved when Elsa's two cards finally arrived on September 20. In Clara's first letter to Elsa she wrote:

"I received the 2 post cards from you at the same time and a letter from you today at 10:30 AM. I am happy, thank God, that you got to England. It must be beautiful in Aachen. Otto must have been very happy when he saw you. What did he say? And how does he look? I am happy, thank God, that you have a rather good situation with your job. Try not to work so hard. Always be merry and sing when it is possible. You like to listen to concerts on the radio and you like cats. Are they nice?"

The letter continues with references to Elsa's cousins Max and Benno Spielmann and Emma Löff, their father Israel Spielmann, Emma's husband Dolfi and their son Kurtl, and Elsa's aunt Mali, as well as Elsa's left-behind boyfriend Fritz. Clara revealed how anxious the whole family had been, adding:

"Emma, Dolfi and Mali were already very concerned until they heard from you. But because Sunday was in between, the mail was later than usual …

Last week Emma slept in your bed for one night. She was waiting for a telegram from you. Yesterday evening, Dolfi and Kurtl also came. He was glad when

---

13   The Munich Agreement was an agreement concluded in Munich, Germany, on September 30, 1938, by Germany, the United Kingdom, the French Third Republic, and the Kingdom of Italy. It ceded the Sudeten German territory of Czechoslovakia to Germany. Most of Europe celebrated the Munich agreement to prevent a major war on the continent. The four powers, Germany, Italy, England and France, agreed to the annexation of the Czechoslovak borderland areas named the Sudetenland, where more than 3 million people, mainly German speakers, lived. Hitler announced it was his last territorial claim in Europe. Source: Munich Agreement - Wikipedia.

he read the 2 cards from you. And he had some discussions with Fritz. Today, Mali was here twice and at noon [during her second visit] I gave her your letter to read. I told her she should write you a note. Last week Max Spielmann together with Dolfi were with me. And 2 days later, the Old Spielmann. He apologized that he was not able to go to the railway station. Yesterday afternoon, I was at Benno's place and showed him the 2 cards from you. The Old Spielmann was there, too. He cried for joy upon seeing the 2 cards from you and realizing you arrived safely."

Elsa had told her mother that she was working for a Mrs. Turle. Clara responded by telling Elsa:

"I received your letter on the 26th of September, and I was glad that, God be praised, you found a reasonably good position as a domestic. Eat nutritiously, drink milk, and prepare a hot cocoa for yourself every now and then, so that you don't become thin."

Both Elsa and Clara thought this would be a temporary separation and they would soon be reunited. In fact, Clara wrote on September 28, "You wrote that I should come to England. Currently I can't decide so quickly. As long as 'one' allows me to stay in my apartment, I will. ... In any case I will find a way to learn English." Clara thought she might be able to follow her daughter to England and take on a position as a domestic, too – as did other family members and friends. But in fact, Clara didn't have the government's permission to leave and probably wouldn't have been able to get it.

A woman from the employment agency (see page 19) that had secured Elsa's job visited Clara a few days after Elsa had left, to see if Elsa had left for England. Not long after that, Clara told Elsa that the agency had shut down.

By the time Elsa left, life had changed dramatically for the Jews of Vienna, with many activities of daily life forbidden or severely restricted. They were prohibited from entering public parks. Then, in November, they were prohibited from attending public entertainment venues, such as theaters, movies, concerts and exhibits; and they suffered ongoing economic hardships because of the restrictions on their ability to earn a living.

Clara had to get by as best she could on her meager income. Theodore, her former husband and Elsa's father, gave her 30 Reichsmarks (RM) a month. She got another 5 or 10 RM from the welfare department of the IKG, thanks to her nephew Benno Spielmann, who worked there. She was an accomplished seamstress and also took in sewing to bring in a little money.

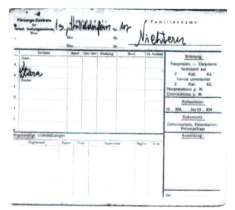

Clara's IKG Welfare Department Registration
(Source: IKG – Vienna)

IKG Ledger Showing Clara's 10 RM Monthly Payments from January 1939 to September 1940
(Source: IKG – Vienna)

Food was difficult to get, too, as the Jews' access to stores was severely limited. Very little was available to them, and prices were very high. Clara was getting most of her food from the Herklotzgasse Kitchen in the 15th District, one of 14 soup kitchens run by the IKG.[14]

Throughout this time, Clara seemed to be the hub of her large extended family and network of friends. Everyone was drawn to her and seemed to rely on her for emotional support. She was cheerful and upbeat and always tried to find the best in any situation. She was hopeful even when hope would seem futile to others.

Trying to make things seem as normal as possible, Clara wrote letters filled with stories of visits and get-togethers – for Jewish holidays and other special occasions, or sometimes for no specific reason. After these gatherings, Clara would write Elsa in detail about the foods they had eaten, the games they'd played and the laughs they'd shared. Without any knowledge of what was really happening in Vienna, it would have appeared to outsiders that life was happy.

Clara shared Elsa's letters with all of the family members and some friends, and they were nearly as excited to read them as Clara was. Sometimes they stopped by specifically to see the letters. They often added their own notes in Clara's letters to Elsa, including offering unsolicited advice in response to things Elsa had written.

---

14   From Raggam-Blesch, Michaela, et.al., *Topographie der Shoah*, Mandelbaum Verlag, Vienna (2015) p 132.

They all also asked her for help. Elsa's aunt, Mali Bader, and a close friend, Trude Atlas, were among those thinking that Elsa could find jobs for them. Everyone wanted to leave Vienna, and they seemed to think that because she was in England, Elsa could somehow find jobs and visas for them. In the fall of 1938, Henny, Theodore's stepdaughter, was also waiting and hoping for documents so that she could go to England.

The Herzmansky Department Store
Source: Die Muskete, 1912

In addition to her family, Elsa had also left behind a boyfriend, Fritz. He worked at a department store, Herzmansky, until he was later conscripted into the *Wehrmacht*.[15] Herzmansky had been "Aryanized" – that is, seized from its Jewish owners and put under Nazi ownership.

Fritz continued to visit the family after Elsa had left. He was not Jewish, but that didn't seem to matter to Clara or to any other family members. This was very surprising since the Bader family was basically religiously observant.

They all liked Fritz. In fact, Clara and her sister-in-law Mali Bader both wrote to Elsa that Fritz said he was constantly thinking about her. On October 13, 1938, Mali wrote, "Dear Fritz loaned me a book. He said that you don't write to him enough. He thinks only of you. There is no more decent guy than he." On October 19, Mali wrote, "Yesterday Fritz was with us. We chatted for a while. Did you have the hiccups? Wouldn't it be wonderful if we were all with you? Not without Fritz! He would be right there with us. It is so boring for him without you."

Clara even said that if she had the money, she would pay for Fritz to go to England! Elsa's relationship with Fritz was one of many topics on which the family members freely offered advice to her.

Clara was also friendly with Fritz's mother and aunt. Fritz's mother sometimes brought food to Clara, and Clara told Elsa how much Fritz and his mother enjoyed the bread that she was giving them from the Herklotzgasse kitchen.

Clara's solitude in the apartment lasted less than a month: On October 1, Clara wrote to Elsa, "Mali got a letter from the [Nazi] Party. … In the course of the next week she will move in with me. But she is fretting some about her furniture."

---

15   The *Wehrmacht* was the unified armed forces of Nazi Germany from 1935 to 1945. During World War II about 18 million men served in the *Wehrmacht*. Source: Wehrmacht - Wikipedia.

And indeed, on October 6, 1938, Clara's brother Leon (Leo) Bader and his wife, Amalia (Mali), and their son, Markus (affectionately called Maxl), were evicted from their apartment and moved in with Clara. They brought Mali's pet bird, Hansi, too.

In that same letter Clara also wrote, "Today in Vienna flags with swastikas are flying everywhere. Is it the case where you are, too?" It's unclear why Clara would have thought swastikas might have been prevalent in England, too.

On October 6, Maxl wrote, "We live starting today with Aunt Clara. We sold the furniture. We are all prospering." But although he was just a teenager, he seemed to understand from the very beginning the urgency of getting out of Austria. He was trying to find a way – any way – to leave. His first hope was to leave on the *Kindertransport*; but, at 17½, he was just beyond the upper age limit. Through a close friend, he tried to get into the Hachshara, an organization that was training people to go to Palestine as kibbutz workers. And, like the rest of the family, he also hoped he could go to England and that Elsa might be able to help him.

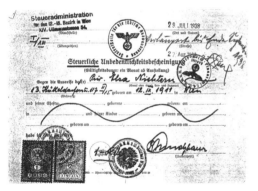

Tax Clearance Certificate for Elsa Nichtern.

Clara's Tax Clearance Certificate would have looked like this.

Elsa was trying to get her mother to England, and Clara was also doing everything she could in Vienna to make that happen. In that October 6 letter, Clara wrote, "I would like to send you 10 RM, but, as you know, I don't have an Austrian passport, and no one else is allowed to send money to you in my stead."

She went to the Central Office for Jewish Emigration[16] and said she'd had a harrowing experience there. But she told Elsa she would go back to the Central Office for her tax clearance certificate.[17]

Elsa had found a position for Mali, and Mali was grateful. She wrote, "I am glad that you have already found a job for me. Naturally, I would ask you to take care of the things. I am happy that I will be with religious Jews. As you

---

16   The Central Office for Jewish Emigration, aka The Centrale, was established in August 1938 by Adolf Eichmann. Located in the Rothschild Palace at Prinz-Eugen-Straße 22, across from the Belvedere Place, the Central Office was established to accelerate the removal of the Jewish population of Vienna through emigration using an assembly-line-like process developed by Eichmann and his henchmen.

17   In order to legally emigrate, a "tax clearance certificate" *(Unbedenklichkeitsbescheinigung)* was required from the Nazi tax authority that certified that the Reich Flight Tax, as well as all other taxes, were fully paid. Source: Reich Flight Tax – Wikipedia.

know, I have only been with this kind of people, so I am able to understand them well." And Maxl added his thoughts: "I am very happy that Mother is getting a position as a domestic, but I would like most of all to be traveling with her."

Of course, Maxl was exploring every possibility of leaving Vienna. On October 19, he wrote, "I received a card from the Palestine office that I should go there today." A few days later, he turned his attention back to England. He wrote, "A person at the KG told Mama that when she is in England, she will be able to ask for me. In any case, I have to know some English, which Tante Clara and I will begin to learn already today."

And indeed, a few days later Clara wrote to Elsa, "I am conscientiously learning English. Dolfi [Löff] has an English book from the *Kronen Zeitung* (the Crown Newspaper), and we always take one or two lessons from it and study it. Dolfi tests us on the material every other day."

Clara was always upbeat and positive in her letters. We will never know whether her cheeriness was real or simply an attempt to put the best face on everything for Elsa, but she seemed reluctant to let Elsa know any bad news.

As the fall went on, the situation continued to get worse. In her letter of November, 2, 1938, Clara said, "Thank God it was quiet in our district, and no one bothered us." This may be in reference to something that Elsa had written, since on All Saints Day there had been attacks on Jews and Jewish establishments by the SA (*Sturmabteilung*, colloquially called "Brownshirts") in Vienna.

Maxl also reinforced the impression that all was well, writing, "Dolfi often plays Charlie Chaplin with a stiff hat and a cane and Tante Clara's eyeglasses. Then he looks as if he was in 'The Sturmer.'[18] Then we fall on the floor laughing."

Then, on the night of November 9-10, 1938, came the horrors of *Kristallnacht*. Of all the synagogues and prayer houses in Vienna, only the *Stadttempel*[19] survived; Jewish businesses were vandalized and ransacked; and thousands of Jews were arrested and deported to the concentration camps at Dachau or Buchenwald. The Herklotzgasse Kitchen was closed for six days after *Kristallnacht*.

---

18   *Der Stürmer* (The Stormer / Attacker / Striker) was a weekly German tabloid-format newspaper published from 1923 to the end of World War II by Julius Streicher, the regional Nazi party leader of Franconia. *Der Stürmer* was known for its virulently anti-Semitic caricatures, which depicted Jews as ugly characters with exaggerated facial features and misshapen bodies. The publication contained anti-Semitic cartoons depicting almost every existing anti-Semitic stereotype, myth, and tradition. Source: Der Stürmer - Wikipedia.

19   The *Stadttempel* synagogue in Vienna was constructed from 1824 to 1826. It was fitted into a block of houses and hidden from plain view of the street, because of an edict issued by Emperor Joseph II that only Roman Catholic places of worship were allowed to be built with facades fronting directly on to public streets. This edict saved the synagogue from destruction during *Kristallnacht* in November 1938, since the synagogue could not be destroyed without setting on fire the buildings to which it was attached. The *Stadttempel* was the only synagogue in the city to survive World War II. All of the other 93 synagogues and Jewish prayer-houses in Vienna were destroyed during *Kristallnacht*. Source: Stadttempel - Wikipedia.

Maxl told Elsa that there was a curfew from noon to 8 p.m. And, on November 13, Goering announced that the Jewish community would have to pay 1 billion RM collectively as reparation for the destruction of *Kristallnacht*.

But, astonishingly, Clara still downplayed the seriousness of the events, not mentioning *Kristallnacht* directly and saying only that the neighborhood was quiet and that she and the family had plenty to eat. In her letter of November 11, 1938, Clara wrote, "You don't need to worry. Thank God, everything is quiet by us." That was Clara's only reference to the events of *Kristallnacht*. This downplaying of the seriousness of this horrific event was a pattern that continued through all the oppressive events of the next three years.

In fact, the neighborhood where Clara lived was in a working-class section of Heitzing, then in the 13th District. It had only a small Jewish population (about 4%)[20] and was away from the more Jewish areas of Leopoldstadt and Alsergrund, so it might indeed have been somewhat under the Nazis' radar.

Maxl was serious about being ready in the hope of getting to England. On November 17, he wrote, "I am diligently learning English. And Tante Clara and Mama must keep up." Then, to show off his new skills, he wrote a few sentences in English: "How are you? Today it is cold. What have you for breakfast? I have for breakfast cocoa and butterbread. I have for lunch: soup, beef and vegetable. For dinner potatoes and might [meat]."

And still, nearly everyone was trying to find ways to leave Vienna. Some were successful: Henny, Elsa's stepsister, got the documents she needed. (See Appendix G for documents required to leave Germany.) On November 22, Clara wrote, "Today at 3:30, Henny was with me, and I made a parcel that I hope she will give to you. Father waited below by the main entrance and then he came up. Father said that a permit also came for Rolf. Henny said that she will leave Thursday or Friday." A few days before she left, Henny wrote to Elsa, "Yesterday we moved out from Praterstrasse 9/12 – if you want to write to Father." She left for England on November 29, taking some of Elsa's things to give to her.

And – perhaps most significantly – things were moving ahead for Mali. She wrote to Elsa, "Today I received a letter from your committee. I am supposed to provide my exit papers and to write to my future boss. I wrote a card immediately. I will do everything so that when the permit arrives, everything will be completed." She learned in December that her work permit had been approved and that she would be working for the Lux family.

---

20   Jewish population data of 13th District, Hietzing, in 1934 from Kofler, Michael, et. al., *Das Dreieck meiner Kindheit*, Verlag Mandelbaum, Vienna, (2008), p 75.

Elsa had helped Mali with the arrangements, and that knowledge would haunt her for the rest of her life. She was extremely guilt-ridden believing that she should have been able to get her mother out, as well as (or maybe instead of) her Aunt Mali.

Trude Atlas also received her immigration approval and work permit for Britain in December.

Many family members' lives were disrupted in the fall of 1938. But Clara continued to reassure Elsa, writing on December 3, "You don't need to have unnecessary worries about us. Thank God, it is better here than in other districts." She added, "Martha Roth and her husband are leaving Vienna the 7th of this month."

On December 6, Benno and Josefine Spielmann and their son ("little Pauli") moved to 1 Fleischmarkt 22. Their new apartment was near the IKG, where Benno worked. Also, the NS-Authorities were requiring Jews living in the outskirts of Vienna to move into the city. In early December, Israel and Rosalie Spielmann had to leave their home in Kirchberg am Wagram and move into Vienna. Dolfi Löff found a ground-floor apartment for them, which was good because Israel had asthma and had difficulty walking stairs. But Emma's worries about her apartment were eased – for the moment – as she learned that she would be able to stay there until the end of May.

On December 10, Edith (Ditta) Löff, the daughter of Siegfried (Dolfi Löff's brother) and Erna Löff, was among the 600 children on the first *Kindertransport* to leave Vienna for England.

Karl Nuechtern, one of the six Nichtern siblings (with an alternate spelling of the family name), was already in New York City. He was working to get his brothers, Theodore and Julius, out of Vienna and into the United States. Julius's wife, Millie, was trying to get to England to join their daughter, Edith, who was already there. Sometime after the *Anschluss*, Edith had made the journey to England with her two cousins, Dolfi and Fritz Singer, the two teenage sons of Anna Singer, Elsa's paternal aunt.

And family members continued to plead with Elsa to help them get out. Mali, relieved that she had her papers and a position and that she would soon go to England, was at the same time getting more and more anxious about leaving behind her son, Maxl.

In her add-on to Clara's letter of December 8, 1938, Mali pleaded with Elsa for help. "I have received a reply from London about a post," she wrote. "You write about this aid operation for children [*Kindertransport*] to England. I asked yesterday at the KG. There they told me if I have someone there, one should go to the London KG and through them write to our KG that one has a place in a foster home there. Therefore, I am asking you if it is possible for you to do something. Your mistress is very competent in these matters. Because in this way, these matters go quicker and surer. One only needs an address for the foster parents who would be inclined to take in a child. In any case, I am writing the information about Maxl to you. He also is known as Markus Bader, born on April 16, 1921, in Vienna. ... I would be very grateful to you if you could take care of this for me. Then I would have my child with me, or at the very least, in safety. Don't be angry with me that I bother you, but I can't help myself otherwise."

As if Mali's pleas weren't enough, in her next letter, Clara also pushed Elsa to try to help Maxl, writing, "If it is possible for you, dear Elsa, take care of Maxl. Maybe a foster parent will come for him." And Leo chimed in, too: "We are in good health, but we can be helped. I and Maxl would like to go away soon. I don't have worries about Mali. Hopefully, soon she will be able to go away. I plead with you once again to take care of Maxl. It will be easier for us when he is away."

Clara mused about her own prospects as well, saying that she was happy that Mali would soon be with Elsa, and adding, "One has to have patience. I ask the dear God that the same should happen for me." She continued, "I am glad that you are taking care that I will soon go to England. Possibly as a result of your efforts I will be able to get away from here faster."

And Max Spielmann, who was 36, asked Elsa to place an ad in *The London Times* on his behalf to get a job in England. He was a mechanic, but said he could also work as a chauffeur, a gardener or a helper. He said he would give the money for the ad to Clara to send to Elsa.

And in the family's last letter of 1938, Maxl himself pleaded one more time: "I would like to bother you with a question. Do you know anything about my trip to go to foster parents? Three weeks ago, Benno also had contacted England for me through the KG. Possibly, if it is possible for you, I would like it if you asked one time at the local KG."

And so it went. All the family members were desperate to get out of Vienna and turned to Elsa, begging for help. It was unrelenting pressure on a young woman who herself had only recently arrived in a new country to try to start a new life – and it would continue.

1939 – "Uncountable kisses from your eternally loving you mother"

As 1939 dawned, Clara was upbeat and optimistic. She'd been to a New Year's Eve party thrown by Ernestine. It was also a going-away party for Grete Spitz and Trude Atlas, who were expecting to leave around January 10. Clara shared with Elsa that Felix was funny at the party, and Ernestine had made good food.

Felix and food were recurring topics: Felix Atlas apparently was something of a clown and could be counted on to lighten things up when spirits were low. Food was often a topic in the letters, with Clara sharing very specifically what she had cooked or eaten as part of the recitation of the details of her daily life. Food was a constant concern, of course, and also a matter of interest because cooking was a large part of Elsa's job.

Clara sent Elsa a recipe for *Marillenknödel* – apricot dumplings – a Viennese specialty.

Things seemed to be looking up for Clara. She hoped she'd soon be on her way to join Elsa in England, and her letters reflected that optimism. She went to a photographer, Gustav Schubert, in the 13th District at Breitenseer Straße 26, to have the photo for her identity card taken. Leo, Mali and Maxl also went to Schubert to have their photos taken.

In her letters of early January 1939, Clara wrote: " Yesterday afternoon [Monday, January 2, 1939], I was at the Schubert photography studio. I had to have 6 photos made on account of the identity card [*Erkennungskarte*] for the Castle Schönbrunn police station … The left ear must be exposed on the identification card photo.

My dear child, I am sending an instant photo of me in this letter. Namely, also the photo for the identity card which every man and woman must have. They cost 6 Kronen and 3 Marks. I have aged a lot since you left me. But what can one do? … That is the way it is with me. Today in Vienna it is like a spring day, thank God. In the photo, I look a lot like Tante Sali. Fritz gave me the brooch that I have on the white collar. The photo is not nice."

Clara continued: "You ask why one must see the left ear with the identity card. We received a notification that the face must be in half-profile;

Clara's Erkennungskarte Photo

equally, the left ear must be in plain sight. The identity card has the purpose – if one needs to be legitimized – so that one immediately recognizes that one is a Jew or Jewess."

On January 13, Clara wrote, "At the same time that I was writing this letter, Fritz came by and showed me the letter you wrote to him. He is very upset. He said that he will send you an express letter. It is not true what you think about him. He is still very attached to you. Otherwise, he wouldn't write to you and would not have had a large picture made for you. Write him very politely and console him so that he will not be upset. He is a good guy. I don't need to write this to you. You already know this. Don't worry about it. Everything will soon be better again." She added, "Sing, be merry and have a good time."

Mali and Leo added to Clara's letter, chiming in with their own rebukes of Elsa. Mali wrote, "I have read your letter. I am very upset that you have written such a heartless letter to good Fritz. You have to make things right with him again and write him a letter saying that you understand you're wrong. Fritz would have already sent you his picture if he hadn't been afraid that it would be destroyed in the mail. Therefore, he wanted to give it to Grete Spitz to bring to you. Fritz was so upset that we all felt sorry for him.

"If one loves someone, one doesn't upset him. So, I have written my views as your aunt and hope you will make everything good again."

Mali also told Elsa that she shouldn't listen to her father in matters of love and that he hadn't allowed himself to be persuaded by his own parents. (This may have been a reference to Theodore's two divorces, the first from Clara and the second from Pauline Markstein.)

Leo added his two cents' worth: "You were crazy with your letter to Fritz … I hope you are calm again now."

Clara reminded Elsa that Fritz would have liked to have gone to England, too, and seemed to have hoped that his aunt would give him the money, but she had refused.

In this letter Mali also wrote that her work permit for England was in Vienna and she would pick it up at the Consulate. But that permit would not be valid – and she would not have a visa – until she got her passport. She thought she'd have it in three to four weeks. Leo was concerned because there were no travel tickets available for Jews right then. In the meantime, Mali asked Elsa to tell the Luxes, her prospective employers, about the delay. She also asked Elsa to get more information on the Lux family, who apparently had children that Mali would have to care for.

In the meantime, Fritz was preparing to go to Germany to report for his military duty. He was still visiting Clara, Leon, Mali and Maxl regularly, about once a week, and was treated like a family member. On January 18, Clara wrote, "Yesterday afternoon Fritz was with us. I was on my sewing machine. He read your letter. The letter was very nicely written, and he was immediately comforted." So, the tension between the two was over.

There were changes in the close-knit network in early 1939, as some in the extended family, friends and acquaintances were able to leave. Herta Fürst, daughter of one of the apartment building residents, left January 9. Trude Atlas left on Sunday, January 22. Then, a few days later, on January 25, Grete Spitz also left for England.

In her letter of January 25, 1939, Clara wrote:

"This past Sunday, Trude Atlas traveled to England at the same time as you – at 15 minutes past half past 11. Mali was at the Western train station, and I sent chocolate along with her. And in the evening, they [the Atlas family] came upstairs to us. They all were depressed as you can imagine, but Felix was again a bit more cheerful with us …

Today, Grete Spitz left Vienna. Mali and Maxl were at the train station and a friend of Gretl – a woman doctor. Otherwise, there was no one else there to provide support. It was much better for Gretl. The day before she was with all the relatives and friends and with that, they didn't need to come to the train station."

Clara gave Grete several items to take to Elsa: a watch from her father, two chocolate bars, cookies baked by Hanni Tant (Fritz's aunt), 10 RM – a generous gift Clara could hardly afford – and the large photo of Fritz!

In that letter, Clara also answered Elsa's question about her finances, writing, "You asked me how much money Father has given me since you left. So that is 30 RM for four months now, in total 120 RM."

After Grete had left, Tante Spitz moved into an apartment building with other seniors, although she was only turning 57. She lived alone in an apartment, but she visited Clara often, usually on Sundays. As time went on, she often stayed with Clara – and Clara had to cope with her as her depression and anxiety grew.

Elsa was still working for Mrs. Turle then, but Mrs. Turle was getting ready to sell her house and move. Elsa was concerned that she might find herself without a job. In a letter written January 30, Clara consoled her: "You write that you will have to change jobs because your mistress will sell her house. One can't do anything about that. Don't upset yourself about it. The dear God will send you another job where you will get better pay. Now you have to speak good English."

In that same news-filled letter Clara wrote that Michel Salter had dropped by the day before and that his daughter had left for England. She added, "He gave me the address of his daughter. If it is possible for you, write her a card so that you might see each other."

She also reported that her friend Martha Roth and her husband had arrived in Shanghai on the 29th.

Early in 1939, there was a major outbreak of the flu in Vienna. Clara wrote that black flags had flown outside the General Hospital the week before, as 80 nurses were sick. And, emphasizing how dire the situation was, she said, "Now they are summoning the Jewish doctors, so they say. Look after yourself. Stay warm, so that you stay healthy for me."

Maxl, who was himself desperate to escape, wrote in February, "Mother and I are waiting for our passports. I have made inquiries to London for a paying position and am waiting with longing for an answer." Still, he was also doing everything he could to help Clara. He had gone to the IKG to get a passport form for her. He said he had obtained the questionnaire and would help her in any way possible.

Michel Salter visited again. He brought along a letter from his daughter; and, Clara wrote, "He was very happy as he read the letter that you will write her a letter. He brought two shirts to patch and socks from his son to darn." The extra income from these little jobs was very helpful to Clara.

Clara told Theodore that Maxl had sent a request to the German Jewish Refugee Committee at the Woburn House in the Bloomsbury district of London – the site of several Jewish refugee-aid agencies – to allow Clara to go to England. Theodore said that he had a relative working at the Woburn House. Clara added, "If you would be so kind when you are there to tell them that and say that you will support me, perhaps it will go faster."

She also wrote, "and don't cause yourself any unnecessary worries about our food. We still have, 'knock wood,' so much that we have to give it away. Uncle Leo continues to get food from the Herklotzgasse Kitchen. Michel now also goes there for food. I always give the bread to Fritz. He likes to eat it, and I also gave him a dessert along with it."

She shared a good time that the family had had: "Yesterday Dolfi came over with a pink carnival hat. He did silly things, and he brought along his mandolin and gave a mandolin concert. And then he put on the wide-legged pants like an actress. Now you can imagine what he looked like! And danced while doing this. We all laughed. And Egon Weiss imitated a cowgirl. He put on your red and white loafers and made funny faces. And it lightens the load." This was a rare acknowledgement from Clara that conditions were not so good.

Plans continued for more family members to leave. Karl Nuechtern, who had arrived in New York City in August 1938 with the help of a cousin, Fanny Garfinkle, was making arrangements to get his two brothers, Julius and Theodore Nichtern, to the U.S. In February, Theodore, who was about to turn 56, had a hernia operation at the Rothschild Hospital.[21]

Later in February, Clara wrote that Michel had sent an application to the Woburn House, but "they wrote him off because he is not yet 60 years old. So, one must have a guarantor who will receive one." She added, "Tomorrow, Saturday afternoon, Mali and I are going to the Rothschild Hospital to ask about Father, and how he is doing."

Maxl had also asked Elsa to meet with officials of the various Jewish refugee-aid committees that were located at the Woburn House to try to help him to go to England, but "I have received a communication from the Woburn House in which they wrote me that I should apply to our *Kultusgemeinde*. But I have no hope to come to England. The only people who can come there are those who have an affidavit for America or a certificate for Palestine. Again, one hope less."

There was discussion in the letters about a wedding Elsa had attended in London, although it was unclear who was married. Elsa had had a good time at the wedding and had met other Nichtern relatives there – the Goldbergs, the Levers and the Rosswicks. [These were the Nichtern relatives who had left Galicia (Tarnow, Poland) and immigrated to England in the late 1800s during the large emigration of the Jewish population from Galicia to the West.]

In February, as Mali's departure was approaching, she became increasingly anxious about what would happen to her son and again pleaded with Elsa, asking if there wasn't something that she could do to get Maxl out. She asked about an apprenticeship or a nursing job. "We don't care. Only he should be close by, or at least in England," Mali wrote. "Don't be mad at me for pushing you, but I can't help myself otherwise." As a mother, she was torn between her own chance to get out and the feeling that she was abandoning her son.

Leo rarely asked for anything for himself. His whole focus was on getting Mali and then Maxl to England. He hoped that if they were both there, he'd be able to join them as well. In his note to Elsa he asked, "Maybe you can do something for Maxl?" And Maxl himself thanked Elsa in advance for her plan to visit the Woburn House on his behalf.

---

21   The Rothschild Hospital, named after its founder Baron Anselm von Rothschild, was the hospital of the *Israelitische Kultusgemeinde* in Vienna, Austria.

Maxl was also more direct than the rest of the family about the increasingly dangerous situation in Vienna. On February 20 he wrote that there had been "strife" the day before, and "hatred has been stirred up," but "now it's very quiet."

On March 2 Clara visited Theodore in the hospital and wrote Elsa that her father was doing better. Theodore and Julius planned to go to England together and on to the U.S. Theodore received a letter from the American Consulate that he would have his physical exam on March 17.

In March, the relocation of Jews to other Jewish homes and collection apartments began, and the city apartment office was authorized to evict Jewish renters from "Aryan" apartments. Whether the family knew about these policies is unclear, but they made no reference to them at the time.

Mali wrote that her going-away party would be on March 20 – Clara's birthday – and that she would leave Vienna the next day. Elsa had apparently questioned whether Mali really wanted to join her in England, and she responded: "You write as if I am not coming. Of course I am coming! I received my visa this week. I want your dear mother to flee with me on her birthday, the exact same day as my farewell party."

In the next letter, she wrote that the IKG itinerary called for her to travel to England via Holland. "I am happy that you will pick me up. It will be a happy reunion," she wrote, and added, "Regarding what you wrote about the silver cutlery, unfortunately one can't take it along. It is not allowed."

Elsa had sent some photos of herself, and everyone in the household – Clara, Mali, Leo and Maxl – commented. "Your pictures are famous," Mali wrote. Leo added, "I was very happy to see how good you look."

In the next letter, Mali told Elsa that she would be leaving on March 22, not the 21st. And she wrote, "Apart from the silver, I will bring you your regular things." Leo sent an update on Theodore. "Your father has received a letter from the American consulate that he should go for an examination on the morning of the 17th of this month. This means that your father soon will be traveling to America, as soon as he is completely healthy again."

On March 18, Israel and Max Spielmann came to the apartment to say goodbye to Mali. The IKG was paying for her trip, and Max had delivered the money to her.

In April, after Mali had arrived in England, the family started receiving letters from her, and letters to Elsa also included comments from and about Mali. Her boss, Mr. Lux, said he would do everything he could to get Maxl to England, giving the family hope. Leo wrote, "So you were with Mali only for a short time on Sunday. How is she doing there? She wrote us that she is with very good people." He added, "I would have joy if Maxl would soon come to his mother. With God's help, Mali will make this happen, and then it will be my turn."

He also recognized that Elsa longed for her mother. Optimistically, he wrote, "So you are happy your dear mother will soon be with you. ... You are already away seven months, and you have such a craving for your mother. Now Maxl and I think about sweet Mali, although she has only been away for a few days."

Mali had apparently told Elsa that money was tight for Clara, and Elsa was concerned. But Clara told her not to worry, that Leo paid the rent and Theodore's support money paid for food. But that source of money would soon be ending with Theodore's departure. Mali also suggested that Elsa should get her boss to help get Clara out of Vienna.

Mali's first position in England as a domestic was not easy. The Luxes, her employers, loved to entertain, and their lifestyle made hard work for Mali. They had 25 people for the Passover Seder. Clara told Elsa that "you can't imagine how much work she had."

Besides entertaining at home, the Luxes also loved to party and often stayed out till early in the morning and slept till noon. This schedule made it hard for Mali to clean the house. She told Leo she was making 15 shillings a week, and that she felt isolated and overworked. Leo asked Elsa if she could find a position for Mali closer to her and to Grete Spitz.

Maxl continued frantically to pursue any avenue to get out of Vienna. He saw two primary options: going to England to be with his mother or going to Palestine. He was somewhat skeptical of Mr. Lux's promise to get him to England, although Mali had asked him to send her his passport photo and health certificate.

He seemed to think he had a better chance of getting to Palestine. He was trying to find a way to get to Paris and join his friend Meierl and go on from there to Palestine, where Meierl's brother was already living. But Maxl couldn't make the trip happen.

Later, in June, he received a card from Meierl, who said he was leaving Italy for Palestine. Maxl's hopes were dashed again, as he lamented to Elsa, "I am a very unlucky person" and pleaded with her once more to help him get to England, writing, "You know what is going on and are well aware one must organize something." He became more and more hopeless because it was confirmed that, with the exception mainly of women domestic servants, no one was being allowed into England except persons who had a transit visa to the United States or a certificate to go to Palestine.

As time went on, there were some signs that Clara saw life getting more precarious. She mentioned that more Jews were leaving Vienna. She also wrote that she would follow Elsa's advice and give Fritz their jewelry to hide, revealing how much they still trusted Fritz. At the same time, she reassured Elsa that she shouldn't worry unnecessarily and that, "thank God," everything was calm where she lived.

Fritz and Maxl sometimes hung out together. They went to the movies to see "Sergeant Berry" with Hans Alber. Maxl said he hadn't been to many movies because, officially, Jews weren't allowed to go to public meeting places. On March 5, Maxl also went to the *Stadtkino* (City Cinema) to see "Four Men and a Prayer" with David Niven and Loretta Young.

Clara still believed she'd soon be in England, reunited with Elsa and with a job waiting for her. She mentioned that the timing was good because she thought Theodore would soon be leaving. He had still been giving her 30 RM a month, and "once Father leaves, I will no longer have money to live on." She also commented that she could be very frugal and was often able to save some of that money. Theodore had also helped pay off Elsa's bill with Protowinsky, the dentist she'd seen before leaving Vienna.

On April 1, Theodore visited Clara, gave her 30 RM, and said he would be leaving Vienna soon. A few days later he went to the *Rathaus* (City Hall) to petition for an extension of his tax clearance certificate. Because of his surgery, he'd been unable to leave during the timeframe of his first certificate, which was typically valid for a month. He was able to leave in early May with a transit visa to England. He stayed there only briefly and was on his way to the U.S., leaving from Liverpool with his third wife, Olga, on May 6.

Clara's determined optimism continued into spring. On April 3 she reported that everything with the apartment was the same and she had no complaints. She said no one had asked about the apartment – possibly a reference to Jewish tenants being evicted from their apartments, which were then taken over by non-Jews. She also wrote that the other tenants in the building were treating her well.

Clara picked up her *Kennkarte* (identification papers) at the Schönbrunn police station in April. She said she would go to Eduardkleingasse for her passport and tax clearance certificate, and she hoped that she would be able to get them later that month.

In mid-April, Clara clearly believed she'd soon be able to get out of Vienna. Thinking she might be able to make some extra money with her sewing skills, she planned to take her sewing machine with her to England. She also started asking around about selling her furniture. In her letter of April 19, Clara said, "Regarding the sewing machine, I will inquire about the cost to send it. I will do everything possible to take care of my passport, so that I should receive it. But it will take about another 3-4 weeks until I will be able to travel."

The Vicarage as it looks today
Source: www.historicengland.org.uk

Elsa did find a new job. On May 1 she started her new position at the Vicarage at Ladywell, working for a Mrs. Cotter, the wife of the Reverend Claude Rutledge Cotter, Vicar of St. Mary's Church on Ladywell Road in Lewisham.

Elsa liked her new situation; she had some time off each day and was happier than she had been working for Mrs. Turle. But Mrs. Turle was still important: As Elsa was in the process of leaving her position with her, she persuaded Mrs. Turle to consider Clara as her replacement.

One of Elsa's letters had apparently laid out specific instructions for Clara to follow to get to England, and Clara assured her that she would do whatever Elsa advised her to do. She had gotten her Polish birth certificate translated into German and asked if she should send it to Elsa, along with a photo.

She also needed to be certified as healthy enough to immigrate. She went to the designated health clinic in the 9th District at Schwarzpanierstraße to obtain her health certificate (*Gesundheitszeugnis*) and was examined by a medical professional, whom Clara described as the "English" doctor, probably a doctor who had ties to England and possibly had ties to the Nichtern family members who were living in England, since Clara made a specific reference to the doctor. Clara wrote to Elsa that there were many people at the doctor's office also waiting to get their certificates so they could leave.

In mid-May, Clara asked Elsa to tell Mrs. Turle that she wouldn't be able to get to England as soon as she had hoped. She asked her to pass along that she would come later and was doing everything she could to get there. She still had hopes of a job with Mrs. Turle. She said she would know more once she had her passport. A week or so later, she learned that her passport was ready and went to pick it up, but she still didn't have a visa.

In May, with Theodore gone from Vienna, Clara was no longer getting the 30 RM a month support he had been paying her. She went to see Uncle Julius and Tante Anna Singer. During this visit, Uncle Singer told Clara that they would help her with money, with Theodore out of the picture. This assurance set the stage for other Nichtern family members to give Clara money, too, to ensure that she would be able to pay her rent and buy food. Clara borrowed 10 RM from Emma and was then able to repay it after she received 10 RM from her nephew Benno at the IKG.

Around this time, food shortages started to appear. Clara asked Elsa to send her some dried fruit, but at the same time told her not to worry about the family's food situation.

They were still getting food from the Herklotzgasse Kitchen, and she wrote, "We have so much to eat that we give it away." She said they'd even given food and money to a Jewish beggar who had come by.

She also wrote that they had gone to the Gloriette movie theater earlier to see "Bel Ami," and Maxl had gone to the Plötzergasse movie theater. Going to theaters was generally prohibited, but they went anyway. Or so they said.

In mid-May, Clara received food ration cards and instructions to use them. Still, she maintained to Elsa that she was doing fine, with enough money to live on and the ration cards for food. But in June she again asked Elsa to send her a food package and thanked and blessed her for the tea she had sent. In late June, she also said that they had received food from the American Jewish Joint Distribution Committee[22] through the IKG.

In late May, the relocations she'd had to make, as well as the departures of her children, began to take a toll on Tante Anna Spitz. She was hospitalized several times in June, including a two-week stay in the cardiac section of the Rothschild Hospital. Clara said that "she is lying in the heart station in the Rothschild hospital, since last Sunday afternoon … I always pray for her that she will be better." This was the beginning of frequent hospitalizations for Tante Spitz, and Clara often commented to Elsa about Tante Spitz: Either she was not doing well or was not in good health or, occasionally, "Thank God she seems to be doing better."

---

22   The American Jewish Joint Distribution Committee, also known as the Joint or the JDC, is a Jewish relief organization based in New York City. JDC's relief activities, emigration aid, and rescue operations were critical following the Nazi rise to power and the outbreak of World War II.

The warm friendship with Fritz and his family continued through most of the spring. Fritz had brought Clara a flower bouquet, a cake, and eggs for her birthday in March. Clara, Fritz's mother (Frau Kaltenbrunner) and his aunt (Hanni Tant) frequently shared food. His mother and aunt gave Clara bread from the "Aryanized" Anker bakery. Clara also mentioned getting veal cutlets and eggs from them. In turn, Clara gave them bread (maybe challah) from the Herklotzgasse Kitchen and then, after it closed, from the Turnergasse Kitchen. (As of March 1939, the IKG was operating 16 soup kitchens, feeding 21,000 people per day.)[23] Clara also gave Fritz's mother dates for him and said that he liked them.

Clara told Hanni that Elsa was cooking a lot in her new job and was using all of Hanni Tant's recipes. Hanni was happy that Elsa was benefiting from the cooking skills she had taught her, and she cried when she read Elsa's letter.

Yet, as the months progressed, the relationship with Fritz began to cool. He was still working as an elevator operator at the Herzmansky Department Store. In a letter Clara wrote to Elsa in late May, she said his mother had told her that Fritz had written a letter to Elsa while he was home on his lunch break. Yet shortly after that, when Clara and Maxl visited Fritz at the store and rode up in the elevator with him, they noticed that Fritz was very nervous. They wondered if that was because he was working in an "Aryanized" store and was talking with and serving two Jews.

Not long after that incident, Clara asked Elsa if Fritz had been writing to her – and telling her not to be upset if he hadn't, "since he is a goy."[24] This was the first time Clara made any kind of negative comment about Fritz and the first time that she seemed to care that he was not Jewish. And in June, Leo said that Fritz had not been to see them in two months, although he said Fritz waved to him when he came home from work. He went on to say that he didn't blame Fritz, as he had to look out for himself.

In early June, Clara learned that some kind of application had been made for her in London, probably for a domestic worker permit. She also told Elsa that she would go to the American consulate to get an application form for a visa. Even then she realized that she should have applied earlier – and she was right. It was taking more than two years to get a visa, and the American consulate in Vienna stopped issuing visas in February 1941. Furthermore, there was another obstacle that no one realized at the time: Clara was a Polish citizen and would be counted in the much smaller Polish quota, not the German quota (in which Austria, then a part of Greater Germany, was counted).[25]

23   Raggam-Blesch, op. cit, P. 135
24   Pejorative term for gentile, a non-Jew
25   Taylor, M.J. (2006). *"Experts in Misery: American Consuls in Austria, Jewish Refugees and Restrictionist Immigration Policy, 1938-1941."* Doctoral Thesis, University of South Carolina, Columbia, South Carolina, p. 130.

A week or so later, Clara received a note from the American consulate confirming the receipt of her visa application. A few days after that, she received a notice from the United States Lines, American Merchant Lines. This letter might have related to the purchase of a ship ticket, another requirement to leave the country, although Clara was struggling financially at that time since her monthly support from her former husband had stopped in late April.

Clara continued to get 10 RM a month from the IKG, through Benno, but that wasn't enough to live on. Clara was still waiting for the promised support of 30 RM a month from the Singers, who were apparently trying to secure a pension for her. As Clara needed the 30 RM per month to cover vital expenses, especially rent, the delay in this process left her with too little money to live on.

In her letter of June 5, as she waited for money from Tante Singer, Clara, uncharacteristically, complained: "Meanwhile, you can starve countless times until you get an understanding [regarding the money from Tante Singer]." Clara suggested that Elsa should ask Mali to speak to a Mr. Rudolf and that Elsa should give Mr. Rudolf 20 RM for her. It wasn't clear who Mr. Rudolf was or how this transaction was supposed to work. In any case, knowing that Clara was in serious need of money, Elsa was trying to transfer money from England to Vienna, which she was able to do a few weeks later.

On June 19th Clara wrote to Elsa, "Thank you many times for the money… you should be blessed by God where you go and where you are, and you should stay healthy for me."

And finally, after about three months, the Singers were able to give Clara the 30 RM a month they had agreed to, and Tante Singer told her to visit her the first day of every month to get the money. Clara also mentioned another Nichtern sibling, Bernhard, who had worked for the *Neue Wiener Tagblatt*, a Vienna newspaper. Although she didn't know it at the time, after the Singers would leave Vienna about nine months later, Bernhard would become the next person in line to provide the financial lifeline for Clara.

Location of Clara's apartment, a few blocks from the Schmelz.
Source: Google Images

Also in June, Clara wrote that she spent time outdoors, often at the Schmelz, a large park and parade ground just a few blocks from her apartment in the Breitensee neighborhood. She would take mending and work on it in the fresh air.

She told Elsa that a bathhouse for Jews was planned. It was to be at the city bath in Baumgarten at Hackingerstraße and hadn't been opened yet, but she planned to go there when the weather got hot.

With their sights still set on England and wanting to do everything they could to prepare, Clara and Maxl signed up for an English class offered by the IKG that started June 15.

Near the end of June, Elsa asked Clara when she thought she could be in England and take the job with Mrs. Turle. She also said that right then would be the best time and it might be more difficult to leave later. Clara said she wanted to come, but she might not be able to leave Vienna for a few more months, and she hoped Mrs. Turle would be patient. Clara told Elsa, "You can write to Mrs. Turle, that with God's help she can count on my coming … Hopefully, she will not wait for me for extremely [long.]"

Clara was still trying to do everything she could to prepare for England. She was taking the English classes offered by the IKG at the Herklotzgasse Kitchen, where she had earlier gone for food. Clara told Elsa that people were also taking Hebrew classes. The language classes met weekly for an hourlong session and cost 1.20 RM per month.

In the first half of 1939, two things occupied Clara's time and attention: the belief that she and Elsa would soon be reunited and the difficulties of managing her day-to-day existence in Vienna. But by midyear much had changed, and she saw that it wouldn't be so easy to leave. With so much uncertainty, her yearning to be with her daughter grew even stronger. She wrote, "Even if I could see you only just one more time … I would be content."

As 1939 progressed, reality began to set in. Clara found out that she'd have to wait a long time to get a visa and should have signed up to leave right at the beginning when she had submitted her emigration questionnaire for herself and for Elsa. In her letter of July 1, Clara wrote to Elsa, "On June 27, I received this card which I am enclosing in this letter. You should have registered me immediately on this day. Now it is already past. I will have to wait a long time to do it."

Still, even as her life got more difficult, Clara was first and foremost Elsa's mother. She bought a pair of shoes for Elsa that were to be delivered to Mali by Frau Pinschowsky, one of Clara's acquaintances, who was going to England. Then Mali would take the shoes to Elsa. The shoes cost 14 RM, and Tante Singer reimbursed Clara for the cost.

Clara continued to spend time with family and friends, as she always had. Sometimes she visited them, and sometimes they came to see her. She went with her close friend Helene Diamand to see Tante Spitz, who was doing better after her recent hospitalization and was staying with her brother, David Sokal. After that visit, Clara went to see the Spielmanns. She frequently visited Tante Spitz, who was emotionally fragile and got upset every time she got a letter from her son Carl, who was already in the U.S. Clara always tried to get Tante Spitz to cheer up, mostly unsuccessfully.

Around this time, Clara got some very discouraging news: In her letter to Elsa written on July 14, Clara said that she had received a notification that was apparently in English, as Tante Singer had to read it for her. The letter might have been a notice that Clara couldn't qualify for the job she expected to have with Mrs. Turle. She told Elsa that Tante Singer had a friend, Hanni Steiner, who had been disqualified for a domestic job in England because she was 46 and the cut-off age had been set at 45. Clara said, "She described Hanni Steiner's situation to me. Now they are taking only up to 45 years and she is now in her 46th year. Tante Singer said that she had bad luck." Clara was then 57 and might have been trying to let Elsa know, without coming right out and saying so, that she understood she wouldn't qualify for the domestics program because of her age. She also said that Mrs. Turle was angry because now Clara couldn't come to England to work for her. (See Appendix H for English domestic program requirements.)

Leo had learned that Mali was changing jobs and would be working at the vicarage with Elsa starting September 1. He was happy that she would no longer be so isolated. He also hoped that Elsa's "people" (also Mali's new employers) would be able to do more to help Maxl. Leo was very disappointed in Mr. Lux, Mali's first employer, who, he felt, had reneged on his promise to get Maxl to England. In his note that was part of the letter of July 14, Leo wrote to Elsa,

"Mali will not be so abandoned as now. I had thought that Mr. Lux was going to do something for dear Maxl. I see what he did. They are our Jews – only talking, not doing. But I hope when dear Mali will be with your people, there the master will do more for Maxl than Mr. Lux." Leo said that Mali was very sad that she wouldn't be seeing Maxl anytime soon. He also said that Maxl had an appointment at the IKG to find out about going to Palestine.

It was very warm in Vienna in late July, and Clara visited the new Jewish bathhouse in the 14th District. The cost was 40 pfennig for three hours. Clara said she always saw people she knew there – from the IKG, from the *ESRA Verein* (a Jewish aid association) and from her English class. They all seemed to be having a good time, including singing and dancing. She commented that she could see how many Jewish families with children were still in Vienna. But she also talked about how many people were leaving or had been forced to move out of their apartments.

Clara hadn't seen Fritz for about three months, but in early July she saw him at a local park with friends. Since Fritz was with his friends, Clara might have been reluctant to cause him a problem.

In her letter of July 8, 1939, Clara updated Elsa. "I saw Fritz standing with his buddies on Wednesday [July 4] evening at the Reindl park. I didn't want to interrupt his conversation. But if I would have known that he had his birthday on the 6th, I would have congratulated him. I will send him a card on his upcoming naming day. I took the No. 52 Tram to Reinlgasse and I saw him when I got off at Reinlgasse. He didn't see me. I haven't seen him for almost 3 months. He doesn't visit us anymore. He doesn't look very good. I gave his mother the white shoes from Uncle Singer that you got for him. Hopefully, they will fit him. I think he will be happy that you sent him the shoes. The dear God should keep you healthy … This week Fritz's mother hasn't been with me, but she will come soon to pick up the bread from the Turner kitchen."

A few days later, Frau Kaltenbrunner – Fritz's mother – came to the apartment late in the evening, bringing eggs and cherries. Clara wasn't home, so Leo gave her the bread from the Turnergasse Kitchen. Clara felt that Fritz owed Elsa an apology because he had stopped visiting them. She asked Elsa if Fritz had written to her about some items that Elsa had sent to him.

Clara seemed to try very hard to stay upbeat and positive – but occasionally she revealed what she was really feeling under the facade. In mid-July she mentioned that Millie and Edith had gotten information from the American consulate about leaving England for the United States, and she hoped that Elsa would soon get the same news. She also wrote wistfully about Elsa, Mali and Millie meeting in Richmond, saying that she wished she could have been there with them, too.

As the summer went on, Clara reported on more people leaving or trying to leave. She wrote about a friend, Trude Baeck, who was trying desperately to get her 4-year-old daughter to England and asked both Elsa and Mali if they knew anyone who would take the child. This was a request Clara would repeat to Elsa. Some of the Nichtern relatives were also trying to get Rolf's child to England.

And in the ongoing saga of Maxl, Leo had sent a picture to Mali, and she was happy to see it but was also sad that he was not in England with her.

The IKG had announced that all Jews could go to Italy. Leo wrote that Maxl would soon go to Italy, and from there he would either be able to join his mother in England or go to Palestine. A new chance for Maxl was the family's fervent hope. Leo said there were long lines of people waiting to get their exit documents.

More people were also being displaced from their homes. Clara's dear friends the Atlas family had learned that they would have to move out of their apartment and into a sublet apartment at Berggasse in the 9th District. They would have one room and use of the kitchen for 10 RM a month.

One Sunday afternoon, Tante Spitz came to visit Clara, Leo and Maxl. She was so glad to be with them that she cried. She stayed overnight and was unhappy to leave the next day to go to stay with her brother, Max Sokal. Clara said that Tante Spitz was much slimmer and that the weight loss would be good for her heart.

Clara's life was also lightened a bit when she got a canary from Max Spielmann and named it Wulfi. They also still had Mali's bird in the apartment. Clara found the birds very entertaining.

Now that they were both in England, Elsa and Mali were getting together every Sunday. In late July, Leo commented on a photo that Elsa had sent of her and Mali together. He said that Elsa looked wonderful, but that Mali looked very serious. Mali had written him that she had been in a bad mood on the day the picture was taken, upset that it was proving so difficult to get Maxl to England. Regarding Mali, Leo said, "She does not appear well, because she is upset about Maxl, because it is so hard to bring him to England. I also am upset ... Mali is seeking to get him out of Vienna as quickly as possible. That would be my most beautiful day when I would already hear that he can come to his mother."

After trying every avenue available to him for more than a year, in an August 2 letter to Elsa, Maxl vented his frustration at her because he had not been able to get out of Vienna. He wrote, "I am still in Germany and have waited for almost one year on a guarantor and as of today no one has been found." He railed against Mr. Lux saying, "Mr. Lux, the 'fine' man, is a heartless and stingy man." He went on to say "Now Mama has already worked 4½ months for him and he hasn't done the least bit for me. Also, you knew exactly that the Lux family had eight rooms to clean and the village where they live lies far away from the city. And in spite of all that, you recommended my Mama to [go] there without writing to her [about] what the situation is. I am certain that you would not have taken this job. And also, not my Mama, if she had known. Now there is nothing more to say!"

Leo echoed Maxl's comments about Mali's job, although he didn't lay the blame on Elsa. He said Mali was alone and had to do all the work by herself, and he couldn't understand why the Luxes didn't hire another worker. He also expressed his disappointment – again – that nothing had come of Mr. Lux's promise to help Maxl.

Leo told Elsa that she didn't need to send packages of food or tea. He said they still had half the tea she had sent earlier and that they were able to get what they needed.

In his addition to Clara's letter of August 8, Maxl was still upset and continued his tirade from the previous letter. This time he ranted about Elsa's inability to get him to England. He wrote to her, "I am not upset at all that you will not do anything for me in the future, because if you had wanted to help me, you would have already done it a long time ago. At least, you would have spoken with Mr. Lux and would have reminded him of his promise that he gave to you about me."

Then he brought up another grievance. He described a photo of Elsa, Millie, Edith, Henni, and Mali. He was upset that Mali was behind everyone else in the photo and considered it a snub of his mother. "Maybe you don't find it an affront that you guys … are photographed [in front] and my Mama is placed completely in the rear." He accused Elsa of disrespect, writing, "Is this any way to treat your aunt?" He said he was not as stupid as Elsa might think, "because what hurts my Mama, hurts me." Maxl complained again about Mali being the only German-speaking domestic in a town that was otherwise totally English. He wrote that once he got to England and got a job, he would pay Elsa back for the money she had laid out for his mother.

Oddly, Maxl then did an about-face: A week later, he wrote that he'd been very angry about everything that had happened and had needed to get it out. Finally, he said that he didn't want to be enemies with Elsa.

Once again, Leo followed up Maxl's message with his own, and it was softer in tone. He apologized for Maxl and said he really didn't mean what he had written. But he himself added that when Mali was still in Vienna, Elsa had written that Mr. Lux would be able to help Maxl once Mali was in England. Leo wrote that Elsa should have spoken to Mr. Lux since nothing had happened in the five months Mali had been there. Seeming to contradict himself, he said that Maxl didn't blame Elsa but was very frustrated, and it wasn't Elsa's fault.

Elsa herself was just a young woman in a pretty lowly position: a domestic in a British household. Yet the family back home in Vienna seemed to think she could just conjure up jobs or visas or whatever help they needed. They perceived her as having much more power than she – or anyone else in her position – would actually have had.

Elsa did everything she could to try to help her family; and these pleas and tirades, which she likely understood came from desperation, must have weighed heavily on her.

The relationship with Fritz and his family seemed to be getting even more tenuous. Clara continued to share food with Fritz's mother and aunt, and in early August she wrote that she had seen Fritz at Herzmansky. She had taken him chocolate and had ridden up to the fourth floor in his elevator. She asked if he had received a package from Elsa, and he said no – although Elsa had written that Fritz had thanked her for the gift! Fritz said he would write to Elsa. Based on Clara's more public encounters with Fritz and what appears to be Fritz's concern about being seen in public with Jews, Clara might have had this conversation with Fritz in the elevator, with no one else present.

It was during this time period that Fritz's mother and aunt asked Clara to tell Elsa that when she wrote to Fritz, she should address the letters to Clara instead. They said they were "afraid of the mailman." Fritz's mother said she would come to Clara's apartment to pick up the letters. And even though Frau Kaltenbrunner and Hanni Tant seemed to have personal feelings for Clara, they didn't want to risk the repercussions if the mailman reported them to the Nazi authorities for associating with Jews.

Very shortly after that conversation, Clara wrote that she would no longer go to Herzmansky. Fritz's mother had also stopped coming to get the bread from the Turnergasse Kitchen. Clara said that neither she nor Elsa should be upset by the apparent end of these relationships. She added that it was too bad Elsa had spent money for the package she had sent Fritz. She said that Fritz and his family were overreacting and that everything in Vienna, especially where they lived, was calm and nonviolent. Clara wrote that "they are peculiar people. They only are afraid. Hanni Tant told him with certainty not to write to you. Thank God it is very quiet here. They are making more out of it than it is. His mother no longer comes now to pick up bread. I am not going to upset myself over this and you [should] not also. With God's help we can live without them."

We have no way of knowing whether she actually believed this or was just painting a rosy picture for Elsa.

Clara continued to socialize with family and friends. After her trip to Herzmansky, she had tried to visit Ernestine, who soon would have to move out of her apartment, but Ernestine had been out on errands.

A week or so later, Clara was at the Schmelz. When she got home, Ernestine came by. They took a walk to a park near the Westbahnstraße, where Jews were allowed to sit, stopping for ice cream on the way. They visited with other friends at the park.

Clara had again gone to the Jewish bathhouse and had seen many friends there. She regularly visited Tante Singer, who was still giving her 30 RM a month.

She wrote that she had received an invitation – in both Yiddish and English – to Trude Atlas's upcoming wedding, on August 13 in England. She wrote that it would be very painful for Trude's parents because they could not be there, "but one cannot do anything about it." She hoped Trude would send her parents a wedding photograph.

On Sunday, August 13, Felix and Ernestine Atlas hosted a party at their apartment for close relatives to celebrate their daughter Trude's wedding – a wedding in London that the family couldn't attend in person. Clara was at the party, along with the Spielmanns and Tante Spitz. A cousin of Ernestine had made dessert. At 5 p.m., the scheduled time of the wedding, Felix cried as he said his daughter would be under the chuppah, the Jewish wedding canopy. The family did their best to celebrate a happy occasion from a distance, but how bittersweet and poignant this evening must have been! Ernestine and Felix sent their daughter a telegram and a letter expressing their best wishes, all they could really do.

Clara said again that she hoped that Trude would send her parents a bridal picture. She and Tante Spitz had sent Trude cards of congratulations. She said she was surprised that Elsa and Mali, who were in London, hadn't been invited to the wedding.

That same day – August 13 – Clara said she'd been at Emma and Dolfi Löffs' new apartment in the 9th District at Berggasse 19, across from the building where the Atlases lived. "On Sunday, I was at Emma's new apartment. I was across the street from Ernestine's at Berggasse number 19. She [Emma] has a beautiful room on the first floor with a view of the courtyard. It is very nice at her place. At one time very rich people lived here. They are now gone. There is an elevator in the house. The caretaker is an old woman with a dog. Her father was a university professor. You can imagine the apartment."

Although Clara didn't know this, Berggasse 19 had been the home of the world-famous Viennese psychologist Dr. Sigmund Freud before he left Austria in June 1938 to go to England.

Preparations for war became a topic beginning in August. Clara wrote about an air raid drill that had lasted for 20 minutes, with very loud sirens. Because of the air raid warnings, the Turnergasse Kitchen had started cooking at 3 a.m., and its clients had to pick up their food between 7 and 9 a.m.

Clara found out from Tante Singer that Theodore didn't have a job. Tante Singer showed her a picture of Theodore with his brother, Julius. Clara told Elsa that a Herr Dorfwirt often asked about Theodore. Clara also asked Elsa to send her greetings to Father when she wrote to him. This request also appeared repeatedly. Clara didn't seem to harbor bitterness toward her former husband.

And the relationship with the Kaltenbrunners, Fritz's family, was not totally dead yet. Clara said that she was no longer going to Herzmansky and that she hadn't expected Fritz's mother to come to visit any longer because of fear. But Frau Kaltenbrunner had come to Clara's apartment the previous Saturday, bringing a veal cutlet that she traded for the bread from the Turnergasse Kitchen that Clara had saved for her, just in case.

Clara said it had been washday and that she continued to wash and repair the laundry. She said that it might not look as good as before, but it was clean and in good condition. She did not have either the money or the freedom to buy new things.

Maxl apologized to Elsa for his remarks in the previous letters. He said he had been upset about his inability to get to London and his concern for the hard time Mali was having at her job and for other things that he perceived as slights to her, like Mali's position in the photograph. He also wrote that he wouldn't be able to go to Italy, either, because it had been closed. He lamented once more that he had only bad luck. "Please forgive me for my dumb remarks, I didn't mean it that way. I was very upset. Now I am not able to go to Italy, because it is closed. I am unlucky. So you will understand it, if one is in such a situation as I."

Maxl thanked Elsa again for helping his mother, especially for the job Mali would soon be starting at the vicarage with Elsa. He hoped that the people at the vicarage might be able to help him get to England. And he said that he hoped one day he would be able to reciprocate to Elsa for all she had done for his family. Maxl was frustrated that time and time again, his plans and hopes had fallen through. And he was only 18 years old.

Near the end of August, Elsa was able to take time off for a vacation, and Clara told her to get a lot of rest. Leo also said he was glad that Elsa was getting some rest and was relieved that Mali would soon have an easier time when she came to work with Elsa at the vicarage. He also wrote that Maxl had received his passport and tax clearance certificate and still had a small hope that he would get to England. But that hope couldn't be realized without a permit or a job to get entry to the country.

Maxl was holding out hope that the family at the vicarage where Elsa (and soon his mother) worked would do something to help him. If they couldn't help him, he felt that he would be out of options. "Perhaps your family can do something for me. It is still my only hope. If also nothing will happen, then I really don't know what I should do. I hope to God that something happens for me, because parish priests are always good human beings."

Clara reported on more people she had heard were leaving, by their own choice or not. Four members of one family had left for America. A mother and daughter were about to go to Scotland. Frau Mihaly (Mali's mother) thought she was about to leave. And one of "Father's" friends and his son had been sent to do forced labor.

Clara also wrote about friends who had been thrown out of their apartments and the apartments taken over by non-Jewish tenants.

On a Sunday, August 20, Tante Spitz visited for lunch and stayed for two days. After lunch they went to the Schönbrunn Palace Park for a walk, but Tante Spitz couldn't walk far, so they were back early. Clara mentioned that they had seen Fritz's mother while they were out walking.

Clara said that Tante Spitz was always sad and that being with her was depressing. Otto Spitz, who was in Belgium, had written to his mother and told her that she should come "in indirect ways" to be with him and he would take care of her. What Otto wrote could have been code for indirect routes that Tante Spitz would have to take to travel to Belgium to meet up with Otto. But Tante Spitz said she couldn't travel alone because of her heart condition that had resulted in recent extended hospitalizations, and she would need a companion to travel with her. Clara was relieved on Tuesday when Tante Spitz left to see her brother Max.

On August 28, Clara wrote what would be her last letter for three months, responding to a letter she'd received from Elsa that morning. As the situation in Europe became more precarious, the closings to her letters got more emotional. By then her closing was usually "Uncountable kisses from your eternally loving you mother."

With war seeming more imminent, Elsa had told her to stock up on food. But Clara told her that things were different than they had been when Elsa had left, nearly a year earlier, and now they needed ration cards for everything. Frau Domischeck, the custodian-manager for the Hütteldorfer Straße 117 apartment building, had delivered their ration cards that morning. Then Clara turned around and said that things were not as bad as Elsa thought and that Elsa should not worry about the situation in Vienna. She added that she was always merry and singing and that this was part of her personality.

Still, there were some cracks in the upbeat picture that she painted. When the Pinschowskys had delivered Elsa's shoes to Mali, they had apparently given Mali a darker account of what had been happening in Vienna in the six months since Mali had left than what she'd read in the letters she'd gotten from Clara – and from her husband and son. Clara acknowledged Mali's shock and then, in her typical fashion, changed the subject. Either she was choosing to avoid a truer picture, or she was concerned about censorship of her letters. Or maybe it was a little of both.

Clara also told Elsa not to put too much stock in things Edith and Millie were telling her about Vienna – things they were probably hearing from Tante Singer. She said Elsa shouldn't let them drive her crazy.

On Sunday, August 27, Clara had gone to visit "Tante Sali" – her older sister, Rosalie Spielmann – at the Konradgasse apartment where she lived with her husband, Israel. Tante Sali told her that she had spoken with Emma Löff, who had passed on news about the possible war. Clara said that Tante Sali was "completely overwhelmed by the war mood" that was all around. She also was likely uneasy about a more personal situation: Clara said that the Spielmanns' apartment had been requisitioned by the housing office. They would have to move and were waiting for more information. (This apparently didn't happen, since it was never mentioned again.)

Clara had made plans to meet Tante Spitz and Ernestine Atlas at the Spielmanns' apartment, but Tante Spitz had left before Clara got there. She told Elsa that Tante Spitz had been having seizures and that she would call Max Sokal, Tante Spitz's brother, to check on her. She asked Elsa about Carl Spitz and his wife. Carl had written to Elsa to try to find out how his mother was doing, asking Elsa what Clara had written to her about Tante Spitz.

Clara was still going to her English class and said it was a welcome distraction.

Leo added his own note to Clara's letter. He asked Elsa to call Mali and tell her that he and Maxl were all right and that she should stay calm and not get herself upset. He said that it was time for Mali to leave the Lux family and go to work with Elsa, as she was scheduled to do within a few days.

Clara wrote that she would be visiting Tante Singer on September 1, presumably to get the 30 RM that the Singers gave her at the start of every month.

Without giving any explanation, Clara wrote to Elsa that they would no longer be able to write to her from Vienna. She wrote, "It will not be that bad;" and "The dear God will protect us."

In her letter of August 28, 1939, Clara wrote:

"You are letting me know that I should make food preparations. Now, it is not like it was before with purchasing. From now on, everything has to be obtained with ration cards, and only a certain amount for everyone. But dear Elsa, it is, heaven forbid, not so bad as you portray it....And haven't you seen Mrs. Pinschowsky? What do you think about how gray he [Mr. Pinscowsky] has become, she too? Mali was also quite horrified, when after a few months she saw her ...

Here in Vienna, we have also heard that we would not be able to write to each other, but may the good Lord protect us. It will not be so bad. This morning Mrs. Domschishek handed out such ration cards to each [house] party. Without the coupons one can no longer obtain food. Dear Elsa, you don't have to be so anxious, and you don't have to worry so unnecessarily.

I am funny and I sing, as you know my nature. I don't care about anything; it is lucky for me that I am so predisposed. I have always told you to be like that. So, follow my advice. God will be with us. As he will lead, so it will be. I live very regularly. I have already taken care of myself as much as I can. I will answer your letter immediately, because you are my only concern in the world. Unfortunately, I can't see and talk to you in person. ...

So, is it so tense in London? Here in Vienna, it is quiet. I haven't received a gas mask yet. Maybe one won't need one. I don't know anything about Fritz yet. His mother was not with us this Saturday either. As soon as I find out something, I'll let you know what happened to him.

Yesterday, Sunday afternoon, I went to Aunt Sali's in Leopoldstadt in Konradgasse. That is a small side street off Taborstrasse. ... She is completely overwhelmed by the war mood that now exists. You know the way she is with her nervousness ...

So don't go crazy and calm your nerves and don't make any unnecessary worries for yourself. I will take care of myself ...

So, I am closing my writing for today and send you greetings and a thousand times kisses.

Your eternally loving you Mother."

And indeed, the August 28 letter was the last one that Elsa would get from her mother until mid-December, as the beginning of the war in the fall of 1939 apparently disrupted the postal service.

On September 1, Nazi Germany invaded the western part of Poland, and Britain and France declared war on September 3. After the successful invasion by Nazi Germany, Poland was divided into three regions: The western region, consisting of those territories along the Germany-Poland border, was annexed by Germany; the eastern region, bordering on the Soviet Union, was annexed by the Soviet Union; and the central region, also controlled by Nazi Germany, became the *General Gouvernement*.[26]

The letters resumed with one that Clara wrote December 18, and she seemed to pick up the conversational thread as if there had been no interruption. The letter of December 18 was the next letter in Elsa's bundle of letters, and it seems unlikely that she wouldn't have saved any earlier ones along with the rest of the collection.

Clara immediately addressed Elsa's anxiety: "You don't need to have any unnecessary worries over us and don't tremble. Thank God we are doing well and always wish to hear the same from you." Then Clara changed the conversation.

Clara said she was glad that "Father" was doing well. She also asked about Uncle Karl, Uncle Julius, and Millie and Edith. It sounded as if they were in the U.S. already. She also mentioned that on January 16, 1940, she and Theodore would have had their 30th wedding anniversary – a rather odd and sentimental comment, since they had been divorced for 18 years! As in earlier letters, she still seemed to have more warmth than anger toward her former husband.

---

26   The *General Gouvernement*, the General Government for the Occupied Polish Region, was a Nazi-German zone of occupation in central Poland that was established after the invasion of Poland. Initially, its towns and villages served as a site for deported Jews from Western Europe, which morphed into ghettos that were later liquidated.

Elsa had written a note to Fritz and sent it to Clara to deliver. Clara said that she had taken it to him. She had seen Fritz after not having seen or spoken with him for a long time. She said that he looked good. However, Fritz told Clara he would never visit again and that he would send the details in a letter to Elsa. Clara also said that Fritz's mother was going to bring food to them, along with a letter that Fritz had written, so the family could add to it (and probably so Clara would send it).

Clara told Elsa that she blessed her every night before she went to sleep, as she had always wished her a good night's sleep and that she'd wished they'd also be together for Chanukah, which had just passed. She said she hoped that "the dear God should help me be together with you next year."

Clara said that Israel Spielmann had come by and she had mended his jacket. He had given her a tip, and he had also given Leo some money to live on.

Leo added his own message, mostly talking about Mali. He said she looked good in a picture Elsa had sent, and also that he and Maxl thought about her all the time and that they were happy she could go to a movie.

And finally, Maxl weighed in. His message was directed at Mali, so it seemed that she and Elsa were sharing the letters. In the last letter of 1939, a letter that Maxl wrote to his mother, he wrote, "Perhaps soon I will be going to Palestine with the entire Spielmann family (therefore, also with Benno, Pepi, etc.). Father [Leo] may also be able to come. I hope that [in the next letter] I will be able to write to you in more detail." We don't know why he seemed to feel so certain of this plan, when just a short time before, everything had been so up in the air.

He told Mali to enjoy herself as much as she could. "You, sweet Mama, are completely correct that you are merry." He said that all the relatives were in good health and sent greetings to Elsa. "We are all thank God healthy, and everything is as before."

As 1939 drew to a close, the little family group at Hütteldorfer Straße 117, especially Clara, seemed to be trying to cling to optimism. Although there were no bullets flying, every day it became clearer that the world around them had become ever more threatening.

1940 – "We would like to have the good times back"

On January 5, Elsa received her immigration visa from the U.S. consulate in London. (See Appendix I for U.S. immigration policy and Appendix J for documents required to enter the U.S.) On February 6, she received her exit visa to leave England and enter the U.S. It was valid until March 6. On February 16, she left Liverpool for the U.S. on the SS Newfoundland. She arrived in Boston on March 3 and from there went to New York. Elsa went from being 900 miles away from Clara in London to being 4,220 miles away in New York City.

Clara's first letter of 1940 was dated February 8, 1940. Maxl's written words attached to this letter were: "We would like to have the good times back!" This, an unusually frank comment, exemplified the upcoming year and the events that followed.

Clara's letter of February 8 arrived around the time Elsa had left the vicarage. This caused a mail mix-up since the letter then had to be sent on to New York City.

When Elsa arrived in New York, she lived with Theodore for eight days. Then she went to work for Julius Garfinkle and his wife, Fanny, as a live-in maid. The entire Garfinkle family was very kind to Elsa. Julius, who was in the garment business, eventually helped Elsa get a job at Howard Clothes in Brooklyn.

Julius Garfinkle was the person who had made it possible for Karl Nuechtern, the first of the Nichtern brothers, to come to America. Julius Nichtern and Theodore Nichtern then followed. Julius Garfinkle got affidavits for all the Nichtern family members. His wife, Fanny, was their first cousin on their mother's side. Fanny's father, Abraham Mann, was the brother of their mother, Eva Chane Sara Nichtern, born Mann.

Clara's next letter was dated April 11. Elsa's first letter and a postcard that she had sent when she arrived in New York City had not yet arrived when Clara received her second letter. Elsa's earlier letter and postcard to Clara didn't arrive until almost a month later.

Clara wrote:

"I received your longed-for letter at 4 p.m. this afternoon and read it with great joy. Unfortunately, I haven't received the card and the first letter. I am happy to hear that, thank God, you arrived safely and that everything is good. Do you have a job as a cook?

"Thank the Dear God that you got across in good health and that everything is going well for you ... You will be fortunate and happy in America ... enjoy yourself..." and "see everything that it is possible to see ... I wish that I would have been able to travel with you, but things don't always go the way one wants them to go ..." Clara added, "Thank God I can still stay in my apartment ..."

Clara continued to tell Elsa not to make big worries for herself, essentially saying it was the way it was and that Elsa should not make herself sick over something she couldn't do anything about.

In Elsa's letter, she sent her mother belated birthday wishes on her 58th birthday, which had been on March 20. In Clara's response to Elsa, she mentioned a party that the family had given her and told Elsa that "I received four birthday cards from Emma, Spitz Anna, Frau Diamant, and Frau Mihaly. Emma visited me on March 20 in the afternoon and brought desserts... We spoke about you. You surely must have had the hiccups. They all send greetings and kisses."

Clara went on to speak about Tante Spitz, whose birthday was 2 weeks earlier. "I will convey your greetings and kisses to Tante Spitz. Her health is not doing especially well. She spent another 3 weeks at the Rothschild Hospital. One must always rescue her. One must thank God that she is still alive. She had her 58th birthday on the 7th of March. I brought a bunch of flowers. She greets and kisses you."

Now that Elsa was in the U.S., all the family members still thought that she had the connections to get them out of Vienna. This belief continued to play out during the next two years as conditions for the Jews in Vienna continued to deteriorate and the desperation to escape grew.

For instance, once Maxl realized that Palestine was probably closed to him, he asked Elsa if she could obtain affidavits for him, Leo and Clara. He reminded Elsa that they had been registered with the American consulate since July 1939, which we know now was too late. Clara also conveyed messages from the Spielmanns and the Löffs, asking Elsa for her help to get them out of the Reich.

Felix, Ernestine, Herta and Titta Atlas were supposed to leave Vienna on March 16, but the trip was postponed for more than a month. Four weeks earlier, the family had received affidavits from the U.S. Clara and other close family friends and relatives had a farewell gathering on Sunday afternoon, March 21. Frau Baron, a close friend of Ernestine, and an unnamed cousin of Ernestine also were there, as well as other people from the Berggasse address where Felix and Ernestine and their family lived. Emma, Dolfi and Kurtl Löff, who lived in the apartment building across the street, the former residence of Sigmund Freud, came over as well. To add some cheerfulness to the farewell, Dolfi put on the pink ballerina pants that he had worn at a party a few years earlier when he had done a Charlie Chaplin imitation and they all had laughed.

After a month of high anxiety because of the delay, the Atlas family finally left Vienna at 10 p.m. on April 27. They took the south train to Genoa to visit with Felix's brother, Moritz. From Genoa they traveled by ship to the U.S. Clara gave them Elsa's address; they said that they would look her up once they got to New York City, and they did.

Early in the year, transports to Palestine were put on hold, only to be discontinued several months later, closing another escape route for Viennese Jews. Under the guise of Hachshara agricultural training for resettlement to Palestine, a few months later the IKG, directed by the Central Office, restarted agricultural training facilities. In May, Maxl was sent to the Hachshara Sandhof camp[27] by Waidhofen on the Ybbs River to do agricultural field work. He might have hoped that with his chances to get out of the Reich fading, the agricultural work at Sandhof would help him get the agricultural training he needed to get to Palestine.

This is how Clara described Maxl's assignment to Sandhof in her letter of Wednesday, May 22, 1940. "Since this past Sunday Maxl Bader traveled with a group of teenagers from Hachshara to do field work at Waidhofen on the Ybbs. I received a letter from him yesterday. He immediately received shoes and work clothing. And the main thing is the very good air. It is an estate. He is doing very well, and it is very airy there. They sing and play instruments there, and he gets money."

But Clara was mistaken and Maxl was probably trying to keep the facts from Leon and Clara. His statements were a distortion of reality. In 1940, the camp was managed by the Central Office as a forced-labor camp with Nazi SS troops as camp guards. It was hard agricultural work; the food rations were minimal; and there wasn't the agricultural training that Maxl expected. It was forced labor, with the agricultural products going to the Nazis.

---

27   The Sandhof agricultural retraining camp was located in the Sandhof estate in Windhag near Waidhofen an der Ybbs. Originally proclaimed as a camp to prepare Jewish emigrants from Vienna for their life in their destination country, especially Palestine, it was more like a labor camp in which conditions similar to concentration camps prevailed. Source: Sandhof retraining camp - zxc.wiki

Clara continued to make monthly visits to Tante Anna Singer's apartment in the 18th District at Weimarerstraße 22 to get the 30 RM from her, which Clara mainly used to pay her rent. But that was about to change. Normally, Clara would meet only with Anna and Julius Singer. However, Uncle Bernhard, who was living with the Singers, was also at the February meeting. In March, when Clara again made the trip to the Singers' apartment for her 30 RMs, she found out that Anna, Julius and their daughter, Eva, had left Vienna and traveled to Trieste, where they stayed for two weeks. Then the Singers left Trieste by ship on April 4 and arrived in New York City on April 18.

After the departure of the Singers, Uncle Bernhard took on the role of providing Clara's 30 RM monthly stipend. Immediately after Clara started to receive her money from him, she asked Elsa to send a card to Uncle Bernhard to thank him for the money and to cheer him up now that all his siblings and their family members, except Rolf, were gone from Vienna.

Uncle Bernhard also gave Clara sewing and washing work to supplement her income. The work from Uncle Bernhard, as well as sewing work from friends and acquaintances, provided additional money for food, and Clara commented that she could prepare better food from her sources than what she picked up from the Turnergasse Kitchen. She said that people were always good to her. Clara said that her health was still good, and she gave some credit for that to the *Wechseltee* – the sour cherry tea that she regularly drank – and told Elsa that "thank God" they had enough to eat.

As 1940 progressed, life continued to get more insecure, both in Vienna and in the larger world. In early May, the NS authorities put greater emphasis on forbidding Jews from being in public parks. On May 10, Germany invaded Belgium and France.

Also in May, Uncle Bernhard found out that he had to vacate the Singer apartment, probably because it had been "Aryanized." He moved to the Gersthof section of Währing, close to where the Singers had previously lived. Clara also continued to receive monthly payments of 10 RMs in welfare from the IKG through Benno Spielmann. Elsa told Clara that she had started a bank account to save money so that Clara could come to the U.S.

It was around this time that Clara finally came to the stunning realization that the date she had registered with the American Consulate for her visa to go to America, June 14, 1939, was a year too late. At the time, it was taking two to three years for a German citizen, including Austrians, to get a visa – and Clara was not considered a German citizen.

Clara had a Polish birth certificate; she would have been considered a Polish citizen and would have been placed on the Polish quota, which was 6,524 for about 3.5 million Jews, compared to 27,370 for Germany (including Austria),[28] whose Jewish population was about one-fifth of Poland's Jewish population. This distinction apparently was not well understood by Elsa or by Clara at the time, because not only was Elsa trying to establish some level of financial support for Clara by opening a bank account for her, but Elsa was also actively pursuing an affidavit for Clara – although we know now that even with an affidavit, Clara probably would not have been able to obtain a visa to come to the U.S.

From April through June, Tante Spitz, who had a heart condition and had had a severe nervous breakdown due to extreme depression and anxiety, was once again in and out of the Rothschild hospital. It was clear that Tante Spitz's health was extremely poor. In fact, Tante Spitz was in such bad shape that Clara described one incident by saying that "One must thank God that she is still alive." On one such visit by Clara and Tante Spitz's brother, Max Sokal, who had brought along a Mother's Day card from Carl and Otto with a photo of them, Tante Spitz broke down in a crying frenzy. During the period of her hospitalization, and in general every time Clara spoke about Tante Spitz, Clara would always provide her standard comment: "Today Tante Spitz was doing a little better, thank God."

In May 1940, the Nazis issued strict rules for the censorship of mail. The new rules required that all letters had to be easy to read. It was also thought that Hitler considered the stylized, somewhat difficult-to-read Gothic penmanship known as *Kurrentschrift*, used by many – especially elderly – Jews, as Jewish writing and wanted it eliminated. Clara, who had spent her entire life writing in *Kurrentschrift*, had to learn to write her letters only in *Lateinschrift*, the more modern German penmanship.

June 11 was the date of the first letter Clara wrote in *Lateinschrift*; and from then on, all of her letters were written in *Lateinschrift*. Clara wrote to Elsa, "Now I have to write everything in *Latein* instead of *Kurrent*. I liked to write in *Kurrent*. But that means nothing. The main thing is that you can read it and you get my letters."

Also starting in June, letters to the U.S. were first sent to Berlin for censorship before being sent to the United States. Censor numbers regularly appeared on all of Clara's letters from June 11 on.

---

28   Page 103. Table No. 104. - Immigration and Quotas Allotted...by Country of Birth...June 30, 1925 to 1938. Source: Immigration and Naturalization Service; Annual Report. Found at https://fraser.stlouisfed.org.

In June, the weather was nice in Vienna with warm, sunny days. It was very agreeable to Clara. Clara told Elsa that she tried to go to the Schmelz, the large park and military parade ground a few blocks from her apartment, every day and work on her sewing.

She felt good when she could get some fresh air. Her best friend, Helene Diamand, visited Clara every Sunday afternoon. Helene always read Elsa's letters. Helene was able to get mail from America from her brother, Adolf Bergoffen, who had left Vienna in August 1938 and had emigrated to New York City.

It was during this time that more Jews from the neighborhood were being relocated to "Jewish homes." Clara remarked that "thank God" she could stay in her apartment, and she hoped that it would stay that way. She also said that she prayed for Elsa during every Friday night's Shabbat candle-lighting.

The Battle of Britain began in earnest in July and lasted through the end of October. (However, the heavy bombing of London, The Blitz, continued through mid-May 1941.) From that point on, mail between England and Vienna through normal channels basically ceased. This break in communication caused all kinds of anxieties among Clara's relatives and friends who had family members in England. Mail got to Vienna through a third party. Mail from England was sent to a neutral country, like the United States, and then on to Vienna. It took mail about a month to get from the U.S. to Vienna.

Elsa became the conduit for mail from relatives in England to Viennese relatives and friends. Letters, notes and photos were sent to Elsa. She then enclosed them with her letters and sent them on to Vienna, usually to Clara. In one of the letters, Elsa enclosed a dollar bill hidden inside a piece of paper, prompting Clara to pray for Elsa's good fortune and make a wish that Elsa would earn hundreds of dollar bills. Clara told Elsa that she cried for joy every time a letter from Elsa arrived, but then added that she should not cry, she should be happy and sing.

With the Nazi invasion of the European lowlands, the fear of a Fifth Column had swept through England. This resulted in a somewhat hysterical identification of the German and Austrian refugees who had fled the Nazi oppression as "enemy aliens."[29] From late May through late June 1940, England arrested

---

29   With the declaration of war on September 3, 1939, some 70,000 UK resident Germans and Austrians became classed as enemy aliens. Some 120 tribunals were established, assigned to different regions of the UK, especially in the area around London, where many Germans and Austrians resided. By February 1940 nearly all the tribunals had completed their work. Many of the aliens were interned in camps across the UK, especially on the Isle of Man. By May 1940, with the risk of German invasion high, an additional 8,000 Germans and Austrians resident in the Southern tip of England were interned. By end-1941 many of the enemy aliens that were interned had been released. However, fewer than 5,000 remained interned, mainly on the Isle of Man, for most of the duration of the war.
Source: Collar the lot! Britain's policy of internment during the Second World War - The National Archives blog.

31,000 Austrian and German men and women as "enemy aliens." Four thousand women and 14,000 men were sent to the Isle of Man. Several thousand were sent to Canada.

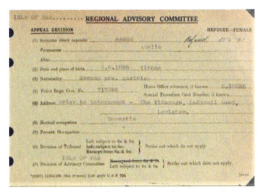

Interned on the Isle of Man Source: https//search. findmypast.co.uk

During late May 1940, Mali, who had been working at the Ladywell Vicarage, was arrested. She was then put in front of a review tribunal, declared an "enemy alien" and interned at the Rushen Camp at Port Erin on the Isle of Man on May 30, 1940.

Grete Spitz, Michel Salter's daughter Liesel, and Trude Atlas, all of whom were working as domestics, apparently were not interned on the Isle of Man. However, like Mali, they had mail issues that caused high anxiety for their families and friends.

The month of July started off with little Pauli's ninth birthday on July 1. His mother, Josefine, had a birthday party for him. Clara and the other Bader relatives, including the Löffs, the Spielmanns and Tante Anna Spitz, as well as close family friends, were there.

About Pauli's birthday party Clara wrote, "on July 1, Paul Spielmann had his 9th birthday. He should stay healthy together with his parents and grandmother. She [Josefine] made a snack for the children. She sends you greetings."

Also in July, Maxl returned from the Hachshara camp where he had been since May. Maxl had learned a lot while at the camp. It was Nazi-administered forced labor and not a good time out in the fresh air of the countryside learning about agriculture.

Maxl recognized that the situation in Vienna was only going to get worse. Immediately upon his return, he entreated Elsa to get affidavits for him, Leon and Clara. He added that someone in America would sponsor them, since earlier it had been possible to find people who were willing to provide affidavits for those trying to escape Nazi persecution.

In an add-on to Clara's letter of August 5, 1940, Maxl told Elsa, "recently I wrote you about an affidavit for me. I could use one. It doesn't have to be strong – only that I have one. Please, if it is possible for you. You will already know. I was born on 16 April 1921, in Vienna. Everything else you know anyway. You will soon find someone. It is completely non-binding. Stay healthy. Greetings and kisses. Your Maxl. " He just wanted to have anything that he could show the government authorities.

Emma Löff had her 33rd birthday on August 14. Again, the Löffs and the Spielmanns, Bader family members and close family friends, like Helene Diamand, were there. Clara wrote about her visit to attend Emma's party. "… we went to Emma's birthday. It was on August 14. She [Emma] gave us coffee and kugelhopf. She was happy that we were there. Dolfi was also there. We spoke about you [Elsa and her father]. I brought her a beautiful muskmelon. Kurtl was together with Maxl playing football at the football field in Ottakring. They greet and kiss you all. She [Emma] had her 33rd birthday. Then Max Spielmann arrived. He read your letter and made jokes."

The families continued to try their very best to keep things as normal as possible. They celebrated Emma's birthday and talked about Kurtl's upcoming Bar Mitzvah, which was planned for the next year.

The following month, realizing that an affidavit was not coming, Maxl changed the conversation from requesting an affidavit and told Elsa not to worry because things were going well for them and they were all supporting each other. Perhaps he was starting to see the futility of his requests and to understand how helpless Elsa felt.

Then, a few months later, Maxl was again sent to do forced labor, but now at the Marchegg camp, about 60 km due east of Vienna on the border with Moravia. He returned at year's end. Clara never mentioned that Marchegg was a forced-labor camp. Maybe she didn't know, or she just didn't want to say.

Clara found out that Herta Atlas was getting married, and shortly thereafter that she was pregnant, and wished Ernestine the best as a new grandmother.

Clara recounted how the departure of the Atlases had left a big hole in their lives and that Felix had always livened things up for them. Clara reflected on the good times that she had had with Ernestine in her letter of October 30, 1940. Clara said, "I had hiccups and my ears rang. One says that when one always thinks and speaks about someone. I always danced and sang with her when she was here. When a Strauss waltz played, we could dance better. We also danced to modern [music]. It made it very pleasant for us. Then Ernestine made tea … It was nice to forget a little bit about the problems, because you can't do anything about them. I sing here often. Unfortunately, I can't be with you. We always played Parcheesi."

Clara told Elsa that she would have liked to have visited Ernestine with Father and Elsa and hopefully, with God's help, this would happen. She did not give up hope.

Clara again referred to the *Wechsel* (sour cherry) tea that she drank on a regular basis, which she said kept her healthy. Longing for her daughter, Clara told Elsa that "I wear your blue work coat for housework ... It is as if I am inhabiting the same place as your body inhabited." Clara also commented on how she always kissed and blessed the photograph of Elsa taken at the Schubert studio before she had left for England two years earlier and "I always pray for you before I go to sleep."

In a September letter, Clara mentioned that it had now been two years since Elsa had been gone from her mother, and with God's help they would be together again by Elsa's next birthday, so that "I will have a little bit of good in my life." In response to anxiety expressed by Elsa because of the escalating war in Europe, Clara told Elsa that she needed to calm down. "Thank God we are surviving, and things are quiet and calm, and regardless, one can't do anything about the situation in Vienna." And Clara added, "One must have patience. One must not give up hope. Hope provides strength!" and constantly reminded herself "Happy is the person who forgets what cannot be changed." Clara told Elsa that she would follow this advice and have patience and stay healthy.

As the year progressed, Clara periodically went to the American consulate to inquire about her visa. She had previously submitted a questionnaire and was waiting to hear back from consulate officials. Clara heard from Elsa that her affidavit had been endorsed and that Elsa was saving money for a travel ticket to America and preparing a room for Clara to stay with her, including a discussion of the room's colors. Elsa wished that her mother was with her in America. Clara then responded. "One must be patient. Nothing happens before its time."

Eventually, Clara was struck by the reality of how difficult it would be for her to get out of the Reich. In an effort to soften this reality to Elsa, who since her arrival in New York had been doing everything she could to get Clara out of Vienna and to America, Clara told Elsa that currently visas were not being issued; it was not possible to leave the country; and not to spend her money on getting an affidavit for Clara because it might be forfeited. Clara indicated that there was no need to rush because everything had slowed down. However, Elsa continued with her efforts to get the affidavit for Clara. At the end of the year, Clara received the affidavit. But without a visa and a quota number, she was not going to go anywhere.

And of course, there was the continuing issue of Clara having sustenance money so that she would have food to eat and a place to live. Uncle Bernhard continued to give Clara about 30 RMs per month, although sometimes not all at once. Clara also mended clothes and did laundry for him and for other friends, neighbors and acquaintances to earn some more money. In July, Uncle Bernhard was healthy, was doing as well as could be expected and was living in the Gersthof neighborhood of Vienna's Währing district, not too far from the former apartment of Julius and Anna Singer, where he had lived for a while after the Singers left Vienna for the U.S. and after his eviction from the Singers' apartment.

Then in early August, Uncle Bernhard had a serious accident that eventually would lead to his death a few months later. Clara said that he was hit in the head with a board. He was hospitalized at the Rothschild hospital.

During one of Clara's visits to Uncle Bernhard in the hospital, she met Jakob Altenberg for the first time. In her letter of August 13, 1940, Clara described this encounter. "I was with Uncle Bernhard yesterday afternoon. He has been lying in the Rothschild hospital for 11 days now. He had an accident, and indeed, a board fell on his head. Thank God he is doing a little better. In the hospital, he gave me 8 RM. His roommate just came to the hospital and a certain Herr Altenberg, a very good friend of Uncle Singer. And he told me that he had received instructions from Uncle Singer [and] that he would be willing to help me when I needed money. I had just read a letter from America from Uncle Singer to Uncle Bernhard. And they all sent me greetings."

From this point on, Jakob Altenberg was Clara's benefactor, providing her with 30 RMs per month.

When Clara first visited Jakob Altenberg to pick up the 30 RMs, she let him read Elsa's letters and on one occasion showed him a photo of Elsa at the New York World's Fair. Jakob told Clara, "You can be proud of such a daughter..." and that "it must be very beautiful there ..."

Uncle Bernhard's hospitalization continued through September, at which point he was released, probably because the hospital needed the bed for other patients and Uncle Bernhard's condition might have stabilized or improved a little. In any case, this didn't last very long since, through my genealogy research, I learned that Uncle Bernhard died on October 16, likely from complications related to his head injury.

Surprisingly, Clara did not mention Uncle Bernhard's death in any of her letters to Elsa until almost a year later. Maybe Clara thought that Elsa had found out about it from the other Nichtern family members in New York, or in typical Clara fashion, didn't want to bring up bad news.

Based on bad news that Elsa had heard about the situation in Vienna, Clara wanted to reassure Elsa and told her that she also went to the IKG once per month on a Wednesday to pick up her monthly stipend of 10 RMs. Clara also told her that she was very careful with her money and could borrow some money from her brother, Leon, and then repay him once she got her money from Jakob Altenberg.

Clara continued to provide reassuring words to Elsa by writing, "My dear child, as you know me, I am not living so badly ... I buy only what I need to eat to have the strength to endure ..." A few months later, with the food situation continuing to worsen, Clara asked Elsa if she could send her some non-perishable food items from America, which Tante Spitz's son, Carl, had done a few weeks earlier. Given that this never happened, one can only imagine how difficult it had become for Clara to obtain the necessities of life.

The last six months of the year were particularly bad for Tante Spitz. She had been in a constantly increasing state of depression and anxiety since Grete, the last of her three children, had left Vienna in January 1939. Her two sons had left Vienna in 1938: Otto to Brussels and Carl to England and then later to San Francisco. With the Nazi takeover of Belgium and the Battle of Britain, Tante Spitz's depression just got worse. During the next few months, she continued to be in and out of the hospital. Between stays in the hospital, she lived somewhat self-confined in an elderly apartment-sharing community.

When Clara read or showed Tante Spitz letters or photos from Elsa or when Tante Spitz got any letters from her children, she would break down and cry. Clara commented "instead of being happy when she gets mail, she cries." Tante Spitz cried and always asked about living long enough to see her children one more time.

Clara told Elsa, "She always starts to cry whenever I leave. She says that she is very anxious about me. She would like very much to be together with me. But unfortunately, that won't work now. She now needs medical help." Tante Spitz understood all too well Clara's precarious status in Vienna and knew full well that Clara had been born in what was then Poland, and not Austria, which dramatically reduced her chances of getting a visa to be able to escape from the Reich.

In her letter of early September 1940, Clara describes a chance encounter that Leo had had with Fritz, who was home on furlough after six months of conscripted military service in Bremen. Clara wrote, "Leo spoke with Fritz the previous week. He had 14 days of vacation. He [Leo] met him by coincidence in the hallway of the Lorzin school ... He promised him [Leo] that he would come to us on Monday, but he didn't come. He looks like he did as before. He asked about you and sent us all greetings. If he would have wanted to, he would have come to say goodbye. He has become a Nazi. Forget him! One can't do anything. He told Leo that this coming Tuesday, he returns to Bremen. A friend of Maxl Bader from Bremen also visited us. He came up to us. He wasn't afraid."

Clara added that there was nothing to be gained over sad feelings caused by Fritz. She wrote, "God is directing your life."

During the second half of 1940, actions were begun against the Jews of Vienna that ultimately led to the destruction of what remained of the Jewish community. In August 1940, Baldur von Schirach became the Regional Director of Vienna. He had a goal of reducing the remaining Jewish population of Vienna. In September, he mandated the systematic resettlement of the Jews living in the outer districts of Vienna to the interior districts. The next month he proposed to Hitler that the Jews be moved out of Vienna.

On November 1, von Schirach ordered that all Jews had to register for food ration cards. With the registration for the ration cards, the Nazi authorities once again knew where every Jew still remaining in Vienna lived. This address update was assembled by the IKG and then used by the Nazi authorities to locate the Jews for subsequent relocations and deportations. Several weeks later, Hitler approved von Schirach's plan to deport the Jews to the *General Gouvernement* in Nazi-occupied central Poland. This plan put into motion the events that led to the first large-scale deportations in February and March 1941 and then the mass deportations to the camps and killing sites beginning in October 1941: the implementation of "The Final Solution."

The Bader family members and friends continued to try to maintain normality by celebrating Tante Sali's 71st birthday on December 2. Clara reminisced about the birthday of her sister Yetti and mentioned the *Yahrzeit* (anniversary of a death) of their mother, Liebe.

As a way of maintaining a positive and hopeful attitude, in many of the letters written throughout the year, as for example a letter in September, Clara would tell Elsa that "with God's help, I will be living with you soon. Then I also will have a bit of good in my life. Only may the dear God keep me healthy."

In the letter of December 5, the last letter of 1940, both Leon and Maxl told Elsa how grateful they were to have received Mali's latest letter, which was enclosed in Elsa's October 30 letter to Clara. Maxl wrote to Elsa, "Many thanks for the letter from Mama. Now we are more relieved." Leo wrote, "I had great joy when a letter from dear Mali was included in your letter. Now I am relieved because I know it is going well for dear Mali and everything is as before."

As the year ended, Clara commented about someone whom Elsa had recently met – a new boyfriend who drove around in a fancy new Buick. As she was closing her last letter of 1940, with the poignant "from your eternally loving you mother," Clara also added "many greetings to your boyfriend, unbeknownst to me, and he should stay healthy." Was this new boyfriend the man who eventually became my father – Joseph Adler?

1941 – "I lived long enough to see my daughter married"

January 1941 arrived; Clara had received an affidavit from Elsa and a communication from the American consulate. Elsa had sent Clara instructions about going to the IKG to make emigration arrangements. As the months progressed, Clara made regular trips to the IKG to find out about emigration. She found out that even though she had an affidavit, her quota number for a visa had not come up. She also was under the impression that if she had a ship ticket, she could get a visa, but the IKG couldn't help because it had run out of money. Without money, it had become very hard to get out of Vienna, to which Clara responded, "Everyone must be patient," wait and stay healthy. Clara said that God would not leave her and that one must wait for the right time.

Clara understood that she needed more money and told Elsa that she would pay her back and said that she was saving everything she could so that she could pay for the train ticket to leave Vienna and get to her port of embarkation.

Recognizing that the IKG could no longer help with the cost of emigration, Elsa was having worries about Clara not having enough money to buy a ship ticket as well as a train ticket to a port of departure. New York City Bank records show that in March 1941, Elsa established a bank account to save money for Clara. Shortly thereafter, Clara got a notification from the IKG that she had received $100 sent by Elsa. Clara thanked Elsa for the money and told her that she was saving money, had enough money for food and rent, and continued to do some mending work. Continuing "My dear child, I have money to live on. I don't pay any more each month. I have sold off various things from the apartment. If I only had the money, I would contribute to the ship ticket."

For some reason, Clara was never actually able to get the money that Elsa had sent; in fact, the money was sent back to Elsa a few months later. In an effort to reduce Elsa's resulting despair and anxiety, Clara told Elsa not to worry. She didn't need the money any longer. She had been able to get a tram card, and she still received the 10 RM per month IKG welfare payment that Benno had established for her a few years earlier. Clara also continued to get 30 RM per month from Jakob Altenberg.

Several months later, Clara finally told Elsa that the IKG couldn't help anyone leave any longer and, for all intents and purposes, it was not possible to leave Vienna. And, as previously noted, the fact that Clara was on the Polish quota, and not the German quota, made it extremely unlikely that she would have been able to obtain a visa.

During one of her trips to the IKG Welfare department, Clara discovered that Benno and Max Spielmann had lost their jobs at the IKG and were doing forced labor. Since jobs for workers at the IKG were dwindling, the IKG probably had a hand in their reassignment as forced laborers. Benno was doing forced labor in construction at the Aspang Railroad station. Max, too, was doing forced labor in construction at Aspang and was also working for the *VUGESTA*, the *Gestapo* Office for the Disposal of the Property of Jewish Emigrants, in a warehouse located near what had once been the Rotunda. This was one of the sites that stored furniture and other personal property confiscated from deported Jews. This property was then sold at bargain-basement prices, mostly to Vienna's non-Jewish population. Little did Benno or Max know that they were preparing the Aspang train station for the mass deportations to the East that were soon to follow. (See Appendix K for list of deportations from Aspang and photo of Aspang train station.)

Remembering the good times and the better conditions under which they had lived, Clara recalled that on January 16, she would have had the 31st anniversary of her marriage to Father: a marriage that had ended nearly 20 years earlier. Clara told Elsa that she had gone to see a movie like the previous year, when she had seen Shirley Temple, and she had had a dream that she saw Elsa, Father and Mali again.

Included in a January 1941 letter from Elsa to Clara was a note from Mali, who had by then been interned on the Isle of Man for several months. Clara told Elsa that all the family members were overjoyed to see Mali's note and repeated what was in the note about Mali working in a custodial job. In this letter, Leon asked Elsa to send greetings to Adolf Bergoffen, the brother of Clara's best friend Helene Diamand, and mentioned that Adolf was a childhood friend of Leon and of Tante Spitz. Clara and Leon, the cousins of Anna Spitz (born Sokal), had been close friends of Helene Diamand (born Bergoffen) and her brother Adolf since childhood.

In January, Clara asked Elsa to write to Dolfi Löff's cousin, Egon Weiss, who had been in the States since July 1939, and to ask him to find an affidavit provider for Dolfi, Emma and Kurtl, since Dolfi was unable to write to Elsa because he was doing hard labor at the Traunkirchen camp.[30] Like many other things affecting the lives of Jews in Vienna, this request did not turn out as hoped for.

As the months progressed, in February Clara told Elsa that she had gone to the Gloriette Cinema with Maxl to see a funny film and a beautiful ballet. Then in March, she told Elsa that she had celebrated her 59th birthday by treating herself to a good meal and going to the Park Kino at the Schönbrunn to see a funny movie. Although it is possible that Clara might have been able to go to the movies, it would have been very risky since as of November 12, 1938, Jews were not allowed to attend movies or other entertainment venues. Clara went on to say that she had celebrated her 59th birthday at Tante Spitz's apartment, where they had a birthday party complete with chocolate, coffee and pastries – all treats that, considering the restrictions on foodstuffs for Jews, would have been difficult to obtain. Was this reality or a charade?

Clara told Elsa that she remembered the good times and the celebrations they had had at the *ESRA Verein*, a Jewish aid organization in Vienna, with two people referred to as Herr Süss and Gilli. She prayed that she would celebrate her next birthday with Elsa.

In March 1941, Elsa had begun a full-time sewing job at the Howard Clothes factory in Brooklyn. Clara reminisced about her own days as a seamstress in a sewing factory, where she had used a machine that was driven by a belt drive from a main spindle. Elsa was using a self-standing electric sewing machine.

Clara wished Elsa good luck in her new job and told her to be careful with her hands around the electric machine. Clara said "I hope that the sewing work is not too hard for you. Electrical sewing with a sewing machine is totally different to work with. You must be very careful so that nothing happens to your hands."

Clara went on to relate her own working experiences when she was younger and had worked with 10 other girls under a Frau Fuchs at Rembrandtstraße 17. Frau Fuchs was the head of the hemming department and allowed Clara to sing while she worked. That had been a good time for Clara, and she wished those good times would return. Clara mentioned that Ernestine also knew Frau Fuchs, since Ernestine had lived very close by at Rembrandtstraße 19.

In the month of February, the first mass deportations of Jews from the Reich to the *General Gouvernement*, the area where the Jews were relocated in Na-

---

30   During 1940-42, Jews from Vienna were sent to do road construction under very difficult conditions at the forced-labor camp at Traunkirchen on lake Traunsee about 23 km northeast of Bad Ischl, Austria. Source: www.nationalfonds.org.

zi-occupied Poland, began. There were five large deportations from Vienna during February and March. Each deportation transport consisted of about 1,000 persons. The deportations were managed by the Central Office with the transport lists developed from the list of the IKG members. The IKG had sent out a bulletin telling its members that they had no choice but to comply with the relocation order for the good of the community, and that infringement would lead to severe punishment.

During the first few days in March, Leon most likely received a postcard from the Central Office, ordering him and his son to report to the collection site in the 2nd District at Kleine Sperlgasse 2, with no more than two suitcases each, with a total weight of 50 kgs per person. So, after living with Clara for two and a half years, Leon and Maxl left the Hütteldorfer Straße 117 apartment and went to Kleine Sperlgasse 2, where they remained for eight days, living in poor sanitary and health conditions.

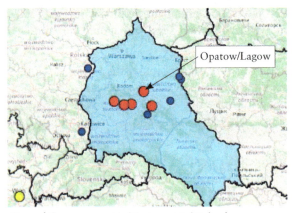

General Gouvernement in Nazi-occupied Poland
Source: www.Neatline.org

Then on March 12, 1941, Leon (deportee #229) and Markus (deportee #300) were transferred by truck to the Aspang train station and loaded onto Transport 5 with 995 other Jewish men, women and children, and deported to Opataw/Lagow, Poland, in the Radom District of the *General Gouvernment.*

By the time Leon and Maxl were summoned to Kleine Sperlgasse 2, it was probably well known that detention conditions were very bad and that the detainees were going to be deported to the *General Gouvernement.*

The deportations were suddenly stopped on March 12 because the railways were needed for a more important mission, Operation Barbarossa, the invasion of the Soviet Union. It was their unfortunate fate that Leon and Maxl were on the March 12 deportation, the final one for that period.

So how did Clara describe all of this really bad news to Elsa – three weeks after the deportation of Leon and Maxl? She said that "Leon and Maxl haven't been with me for three weeks now," not that they had been deported to the *General Gouvernement*. She reminisced that Kleine Sperlgasse 2 was where she and Leon had gone to grade school and that things "went well for them there." She told Elsa that there had been too many people in the apartment before and now, even though she was alone, thank God it was quiet. Once again Clara was covering up a really bad situation and giving it a positive spin.

We get a real sense of how bad things were from Emma Löff's March 16, 1941, letter of desperation. Following up on Clara's request to Elsa, Emma said that she was writing on behalf of Dolfi, who had been doing hard labor, to which he was not accustomed.

The forced labor was taking its toll on him, and he couldn't write to Elsa. Emma was desperately seeking help so that they could get out of the Reich. Emma referred to telegrams that had been sent to Elsa as well as to Egon Weiss, Dolfi's first cousin, who had been able to get out of Vienna two years earlier because he had a relative in the States.

Emma told Elsa that they were notified that they had been sent an affidavit earlier in 1941, but it had gotten lost in the U.S. embassy and now, after almost three months, it had been found. They had obtained the affidavit through Egon Weiss and a man named Asinoff, who was the affidavit provider. But having an affidavit was not good enough.

They also had to have a fully paid-for ship ticket. Without a ship ticket, they could not get a visa, even though they had passed their health exam.

Emma wrote:

"Dearest Elsa

Based on our joint telegrams you are already informed of our wishes, and I will communicate the entire situation to you.

After an endlessly long time the Affidavit from the consulate has been found and the investigation occurs immediately upon presentation of the ship tickets. Now you are, dearest Elsa, the only relative in the USA. And at the same time, our only hope.

We ask you most intimately (I am also speaking for Dolfi, who is working outside [of Vienna], about whom you have heard from your mother, who as a result cannot write for himself) help us for the required amount and arrange the payment at the Joint [The American Joint Distribution Committee].

Your good mother is OK with it. Often, she is with me the entire day. It would be her fondest wish to make the passage together with us. Should you alone not be in the position to raise this sum, request the relatives, friends and other acquaintances to raise portions of the required money.

We help your dear mother in every way until the departure and hope that we have not turned to you in vain. We will of course – this goes without saying – pay you back everything to the last cent. It is completely impossible to obtain a visa in any other way in spite of passing the examination that filtered applicants. Your dear mother cannot accomplish the [ocean] crossing alone – she asks you fervently – you should do everything you can there so that we can travel together. Since it is our most fervent request and also the wish of your dear mother, I hope that you will certainly – as the splendid person I know you to be – help us.

Besides the Atlases, with whom you are in contact, I also have telegraphed Egon Weiss. He would like together with the affidavit provider Asinoff - to deposit the same amount (at the Joint). I beg you to raise these necessary amounts together with the Atlases, Egon and Asinoff and for the time being to start with the Atlases and Egon Weiss.

The hard labor Dolfi is performing – to which he is unaccustomed – is the utmost burden to him. Dolfi's health is not the best. I am giving you the address at the end [of this letter].

Dear Elsa, how are you doing? As I see from your letters, things are good for you, and I wish for you from now on only the very best. Your dear mother is often with me. She is healthy and well. Often, she is with me the whole day and we speak only about you. Kurt and I are well. My dear parents send you heartfelt greetings.

Once again Elsa, I implore you to help us. You are our only hope!

Heartfelt greetings and kisses, Emma and Kurt Löff.

Kisses to the Atlas family."

Unfortunately, Emma's poignant words were not enough. Elsa was unable to help them.

In April, Clara told Elsa that this was the first time in her entire life that there was no one with her for Passover, and then told Elsa not to get upset, because she was not completely alone. She had the cute little bird that Max Spielmann had gotten her two years earlier. Clara said that she was getting used to being alone in her apartment and it was not so bad as long as she could earn some money and stay where she was.

Clara said that things were going well; she was eating good things; and she treated herself to an eighth of a liter of a wine spritzer per day to stay perky. She told Elsa not to lose courage. She finally added, "The Dear God is always with me."

Clara went on to tell Elsa that Leon and Maxl were doing well and were living in a village with 50 Jewish families and had been invited to Friday and Saturday meals – just as it had been when Clara's mother was around. In reality, Clara might not have known that the conditions in the small and poor Polish towns where the deportees were sent were already highly stressed as a result of the Nazi invasion and occupation of Poland, and this stress was made even worse by the influx of large numbers of Jewish deportees from the Reich.

A few weeks after Passover, Clara told Elsa that Leon and Maxl were in Opatow and things were going very well for them and that they were being treated very well by the Jews of the community. She said they had been invited to the home of a local villager for two Passover Seders, which included chicken soup, chicken, eggs and matzahs. In between, they had borscht and lots of potatoes.

During the following months, Clara and Fanny Mihaly received cards from Leon and Maxl. The cards said that they were staying with a miller and had enough to eat including eggs, milk and other provisions. Maxl told his grandmother, Fanny, that he had gone to a Jewish wedding, had had good food and had become acquainted with the miller's 17-year-old daughter, and that a marriage could be in the offing. Maybe Leon and Maxl told them all this "made-up" good news to bolster the spirits of those left behind in Vienna.

Clara gave Elsa their address: Josef Weisdorf dla. Bader Leon Slabliszowice, Post Lipnik Kreis Opatow, *General Gouvernement*. She told Elsa to tell Mali that she should write to Leon and Maxl directly, since it was very difficult to send letters from Vienna to the *General Gouvernement*. Clara told Elsa that Max Spielmann had sent Leo 30 RM but had no idea if Leo had ever received it.

Mail delivery from the *General Gouvernement* was very erratic. There were large time gaps between the cards from Leo and Maxl, which caused great worries among the family members. When the censored postcards did arrive, Leon and Maxl continued to tell the family that they were doing well and were getting lots of sunshine and were heavily tanned. This might have been their way of saying that they were doing a lot of work outside. It was highly likely that they were doing forced labor and were trying to make their situation sound good. Conditions in the ghetto-like towns were not good; and the Jews, especially those from Vienna, had to do forced labor. As time went on, communication between Vienna and the *General Gouvernement* deteriorated even more.

In a March letter and then again in an April letter, Clara described visits she had made to the offices of the American Hamburg Shipping Line, located at the corner of Kärntnerstraße and Ringstraße (the circular grand boulevard that encircles the *Innere Stadt*), to inquire about the cost and availability of ship tickets, which had become the major deciding factor in getting out of Vienna. During these visits she encountered Pauline Markstein, the second wife of Theodore Nichtern – the woman he had married a few years after his divorce from Clara and later had divorced. Pauline and Theodore had no children, but Pauline had two children from her first marriage to Juda Atlas (1907-1919). It was during the marriage to Juda Atlas that Theodore had gotten to know her, since Clara's sister, Yetti, was married to Juda Atlas' brother, Philip, during that time.

Clara told Elsa to convey her greetings to Pauline's daughter, Trude, who was living in New York City with her husband and commented about how well Trude and her husband were treating Elsa. Clara asked Elsa if she had any idea how Pauline's son Richard was doing and asked Elsa if she could send her a photo of Trude so that she could give it to Pauline and expressed the hope that Pauline could see her children once again and that she could be with Elsa at her next birthday – saying "It is the wish of every mother to see her children again."

On March 11, Elsa received a letter from Mali, who had been interned on the Isle of Man since late May 1940. The letter came to Elsa, and she was supposed to send it to Leon and Maxl in Vienna. This indirect method was the way mail had been delivered to Vienna for months. The letter had been written a few days earlier, and Mali had no idea that Leon and Maxl had been forced to leave Vienna.

It was not clear why Elsa still had this letter, which I found in her bundle of saved letters from family members. Was it ever forwarded to Leon and Maxl? Had it been sent and returned? In any case, it was extremely poignant considering that Mali had written the letter to Leon and Maxl for their respective birthdays, and this might have been the last birthday wish that Mali would ever have been able to send them – and that they ever would have received from her.

Mali sent birthday wishes to her son on his upcoming 20th birthday on April 16. She wished that they would be together again. She sent belated birthday wishes to her husband, who had turned 55 on February 28, and asked how he had spent his birthday. Mali said that she was doing well. She had everything she needed except Leon. She asked about Tante Spitz's health, about her mother and siblings, and sent greetings and kisses to all the loved ones, other relatives and acquaintances.

On March 11, 1941, Mali wrote:

"Dear child!

Today I must already congratulate you on your coming Birthday, if my letter doesn't get to you at the right time. God should only allow you to be well my adorable one; everything that you would wish for should come true. What would be my eternal wish, if God wants, will be to allow us to be together soon. Hopefully you are all well.

Dearest Leo,

How did you spend your birthday? It was Friday and I thought about you the whole day. I was very sad that I was not able to be with you. Now only don't lose courage, neither you nor I. The sun still comes [out]; it will shine also for us.

I am doing well. Don't worry about me. I have everything – except for you.

How is my mother and how are my siblings doing? Uncountable kisses to them; and, of course, to all the relatives. Greetings to all our friends.

Is Tante Spitz well? Kisses to her.

So golden Maxl, God bless you and your father and all our loved ones. Kisses to dear Clara and Elsa. Kisses to you.

Your loving

Mutti."

Mail service in and out of Vienna continued to deteriorate. In May, Clara told Elsa that no one was receiving mail from Mali, which made all the Mihaly family very anxious.

Clara received notification from the postal inspector that written correspondence enclosed in a letter was now forbidden, and any notes, cards or letters must come from authorized locations, like the U.S., or neutral countries, like Portugal or Switzerland.

In Mali's case, that meant that news from England would not make it to Vienna unless Elsa transcribed Mali's letters. The same rules on correspondence applied to communication from the *General Gouvernement*, which was spotty at best. Elsa was told by Clara that she needed to relay this to Mali and other family members and that Elsa would need to transcribe anything from Mali or other relatives into the body of her letters in order to get through the censors. She was also told to use good-quality writing paper to facilitate the transcription.

Tante Spitz continued to be afflicted by progressively worsening melancholy and depression. She got periodic mail from her two sons: Otto, who was now married to Cilli and was still living in Belgium; and Carl, who was married to Felicia and had made it to San Francisco. However, there was not much mail from Grete, her daughter in England. Regardless, mail didn't help pull Tante Spitz out of her depression. Every time she got mail or a package, she broke down. Clara told Elsa, "One can tell her 100 times not to cry, but she doesn't listen. … Instead, she should thank God that she gets mail …" Her brothers, David and Max Sokal, stayed overnight to look after her since they couldn't get any female help to stay with her because of her depressed condition.

When Clara went to visit Tante Spitz, she always took her something to eat. Tante Spitz continually wanted to spend time with Clara and even to move in with her. Although she was very sympathetic to Tante Spitz's condition, Clara didn't think that was a good idea because of Tante Spitz's depressed nature. Clara wrote to Elsa, "I have a completely different nature. I always sing and am cheerful and whistle about it." Clara always said that she tried to be happy as a way of dealing with things she couldn't do anything about.

However, in May and again in June, Tante Spitz did stay with Clara. She had been going through one of her better spells, fueled mainly by letters from her daughter, Grete, that were being sent to her by Elsa. While Clara and Tante Spitz were together, they cheered each other up and had a few laughs by talking about the good old times and how "meschugene Felix Atlas" would do crazy, "off-the-wall" things. Clara asked Elsa to tell Grete that her mother's thoughts were always with her, which made Tante Spitz sad again. Clara told Elsa that she didn't allow Tante Spitz to be sad when she was with her.

While Tante Spitz was with Clara, Clara brought her together with Fanny Mihaly for the first time in two years. Fanny talked about a Mr. Fried, who was able to get mail from his children in England on a regular basis through some irregular back channels, and she'd hoped he might assist Tante Spitz with the same. However, nothing ever came of this.

In a story that represented how many non-Jews helped their Jewish friends, neighbors and acquaintances obtain the necessities of life to survive, Clara told Elsa about a woman, Frau Kari, who had been Clara's cleaning lady when she was married to Theodore. Because of the elimination of Jewish shop owners, Frau Kari, who was not Jewish, most probably had taken over ownership of a dairy store and, despite all the restrictions, was providing food to Jews, including Clara. Clara told Elsa that Frau Kari provided her with some milk and other dairy products to the extent possible and that Clara then shared them with Tante Spitz.

Not only did Clara get food from Frau Kari, but other friends and acquaintances from the apartment house and from the neighborhood also supported Clara with food and mending work so that she could make some extra money to buy necessities. This aid plus the 10 RMs from the IKG welfare department, the 30 RMs from Jakob Altenberg and money from the periodic sale of her apartment furnishings, which Clara didn't mention until her forced relocation a few months later, kept Clara afloat.

It seemed that the month of April, as identified by what happened to Clara, her relatives and friends, was a turning point and appeared to be the point at which "The Final Solution to the Jewish question" was put into motion in Vienna.

On April 7, Clara received a postcard that required her to go to the Central Office at Prinz-Eugen-Straße, for what amounted to five hours of probably intense questioning. Clara told Elsa that the lines were long and many people were there being interrogated, including many of Clara's Jewish friends and acquaintances. Clara told Elsa that "Thank God it's over!" What Clara didn't know was that these interrogations were used to finalize the database for the relocation and staging of the Jewish population in preparation for the mass deportations that were waiting on the horizon. Clara's close friend Michel Salter, whose 61st birthday was on April 11, had to go to the Central Office for interrogation on April 9. Grete Mihaly; her mother, Fanny; and her sister, Tini, also received post cards in April and had to appear at the Central Office for interrogation.

Besides Viennese men, like Dolfi, being conscripted to do forced labor outdoors, the Nazis were now conscripting and sending away Viennese women under the age of 50 for forced labor in factories. In a frightening incident that happened to Emma during her Central Office interviews, Clara said, "A few days ago, Emma was at Prinz-Eugen Straße [the Central Office]. They wanted to send her away to work. This made her sick. She had heart palpitations. They immediately took her to a room. Thank God she slipped through." Emma got lucky. She wasn't considered healthy enough to be sent away. Then Pepi (Josefine) Spielmann had to go through a similar ordeal at the Central Office, but somehow also avoided being sent away.

Sometimes the requests from the Central Office were framed as updates to one's emigration questionnaire; but considering the unlikelihood of emigration, the meetings with officials were more to update the files on Vienna's Jews. In a prescient letter a few weeks later, Clara told Elsa, "Thank God, things aren't going badly for me… until further notice [I] am still in my apartment and [can] earn some money with my sewing …"

Clara also continued to tell Elsa about Dolfi's outdoor hard labor, how he was constantly sick, and how Emma was very worried about him. Clara told Elsa that he was working in the fresh air and, in jest, "…in his letter, he sent me a little bit of fresh air from Ischl."

And we finally come to the last chapter of the Fritz story! During the winter, Fritz had been stationed in Bremen and was working as a cook. Before his deportation in March, Leon told Clara that he had found out that Fritz had a girlfriend, who he thought was someone that Fritz had met when he worked at the Herzmansky Department Store.

In May, Clara identified a Herr Wohlmut as the uncle of Fritz. He asked Clara for Elsa's address in New York so he could give it to Fritz and Fritz could write to Elsa. With this request, Clara told Elsa, "My dear child don't get upset because of Fritz. One must forget what is past. The Dear God will not leave you … It is all destiny. I believe that he will not be happy with her, as you know him … You will still find happiness in this world." These words from Clara are the last mention of Fritz.

While all of this was happening, everyone was trying to live as normal a life as possible during times of increasing Nazi persecution. Clara continued to fill her letters with bits and pieces of local information and gossip as a way to maintain some degree of regularity in her life. Pauli continued to learn how to play the violin; and, when they could, Pauli and Kurtl went to play soccer. Clara regularly visited Emma Löff and Pepi Spielmann, and they talked about Kurtl's future Bar Mitzvah. The Fürsts' son, Walter, was living in New York. He was working at a medical factory, was making a good salary and was planning to marry a girl from Vienna. Clara's brother-in-law, Israel Spielmann, had been hospitalized, but now was recovering at home. Max Sokal was attempting to move into the old-age home in the 9th District at Seegasse. However, Max was not able to get into the old-age home at Seegasse, probably because it was already fully occupied, but was able to get into the old-age home at Alxingergasse 97 in the 10th District.

The family continued the attempt to send food packages and letters to Leon and Maxl in Poland but were not sure they were getting through. Rolf Nichtern was still at the X-ray department of the Rothschild hospital and told Clara how difficult Uncle Bernhard had been after he had been injured and that he was buried with his parents at the *Zentralfriedhof* (central cemetery of the city of Vienna). Herta Atlas was due with child in June, and Clara sent her best wishes to the prospective grandparents, Ernestine and Felix.

Clara continued to get food and some mending work from non-Jewish friends and neighbors who, like Frau Kari, were willing to go against Nazi anti-Jewish laws to help her because she was so well-liked. Clara sent greetings to the Garfinkle family for continuing to help Elsa. The Garfinkles had hired Elsa as their maid when she had first arrived in New York City a year earlier. Still thinking that there might be some hope of getting to the U.S., or just wanting to keep up the pretense of that possibility, Clara continued to take English lessons.

Then, at the end of May, the knowledge of where the Jews of Vienna were located – from the Central Office interviews in April and the IKG residence data from the ration-card registrations – was put to use. Alois Brunner, Director of the Central Office after Adolf Eichmann, issued the order that all the Jews living throughout all the districts of Vienna were to be relocated to the 2nd, 9th and 20th Districts. A few weeks later, the relocations began. Probably realizing that she was going to be relocated, but in her typical way of hiding the true gravity of the situation facing her, Clara never mentioned this order to Elsa until a few months after it happened.

In June 1941, Elsa was living with her father in Manhattan. A few months later, in September, she moved to the Singer family residence at 105th Street on Manhattan's Upper West Side, where she would stay until her marriage in November.

And in June 1941, Alois Brunner's order was put in motion, and the forced relocation of the Jews from the various districts of Vienna to the 2nd, 9th and 20th Districts began. This was the beginning of the preparation for the mass deportations that would start once again in October, after the interruption in March while the Reich had prepared for its invasion of the Soviet Union, which took place on June 22. The move to the 2nd, 9th and 20th Districts marked the beginning of the end for Clara and for the Jews of Vienna.

Throughout this entire period Clara's letters included comments about Leon and Maxl, who were still in Opatow in the *General Gouvernement*: their address; their need for money; their need for food packages. Clara continually asked Elsa to try to send Leon and Maxl a food package, although she also kept saying that things were going generally well for them. However, everything that is known about the Jewish ghettos in the *General Gouvernement* indicates that food was scarce, accommodations were very poor, and sanitary conditions were not good and got progressively worse until the liquidation of the ghettos in October 1942. Clara told Elsa that it was not possible to send anything to Leon and Maxl from Vienna and gave their address as: Leon Bader; Cmielow, Koszieina 5; Kreis Opatow; *General Gouvernement*.

Also, in June, Elsa received the first of two typed letters from Carl Spitz, who was living with his wife, Felicia, in San Francisco. Carl's letter of June 21, 1941, was extremely negative about the situation in Vienna, even though Clara was always making positive comments to Elsa, or at least saying things were essentially manageable. Carl told Elsa that it would be a miracle if they could get their mothers out of Vienna and to the United States. His mother always commented on how Elsa was trying so hard to get her mother to America. He told Elsa how happy his mother was when she was with Clara and how Clara was a calming influence on his mother.

About his mother and Clara, Carl wrote,

"I receive regular mail from home and just recently 3 letters came one after the other. In every letter Mother writes how happy she is when she is with Tante Klara and how she always looks forward to Wednesday, when Klara makes her weekly visit. In the last letter Mother even wrote that she went out for her first visit [since hospitalization] to Tante Klara's, where she stayed over the weekend.

Uncle Max, who always sends along very kind and comprehensive letters, adds that 'when she [Anna Spitz] is with Tante Klara, she is calmer than otherwise; and Wednesdays are like a day of recovery, that she can count on.' Mother had experienced nice days in the circle of her family and at times with Klara alone ... It is touching to see how Mother feels drawn to Klara and only to Klara. Most of all Mother would love to have Klara with her all the time. Mother writes in this most recent letter, 'My dear children, Tante Klara invited me over for a few days; I am writing this letter at her place and will get it in the mail from here. Tomorrow I have to go back home again. With Tante Klara I feel quite well. Her calm demeanor has a pleasant effect upon me ...

Indeed, Elsa, how happy we would be, if our mothers could be here with us! Our worries would be removed. But the way things are now, it would be a miracle, if we would succeed [in having our mothers come over to live with us.] With the departure of many American consulates from almost all of Europe and especially with the latest policy proceeding from Washington, the last bit of hope has just about been snuffed out. Even I could not obtain the first small affidavit; (please don't write back home about this outcome, Elsa, n'est ce pas? When I write my mother about these things, I change the story a bit, so that Mother does not completely lose hope and courage) and now just about all attempts at obtaining an affidavit are mainly illusory. I am glad your mother is keeping it together so splendidly. It is fortunate for her that she is holding it all together. And then you also have milder worries, knowing that your mother is managing all right. That must be good news for you. It is really the only possible way to make it through these difficult times."

With the impending closure of the American consulate and the restrictive U.S. immigration policies, there was no hope. Carl couldn't get an affidavit for his mother and asked Elsa not to tell her mother this. He was concerned that communication would be cut off and was looking for other ways to get letters into and out of Vienna, such as through neutral countries. Carl told Elsa that his brother, Otto, was living in Brussels with his wife, Cilli, and that every day was a struggle to survive because they had very little money to buy food and prices continued to rise.

July started off with Clara reminiscing again about her better days when she had worked on hems, seams and borders at the clothes-making factory at Rembrandtstraße 17, was well paid, and had a good boss, Frau Fuchs, whom Ernestine Atlas knew well, since Ernestine had lived at Rembrandtstraße 19. Clara told Elsa that "I wish that it was still like this now."

Clara told Elsa that the Altenberg family had been forced to relocate to Hütteldorfer Straße 70, not far from where Clara lived. Clara said that Jakob Altenberg was hospitalized because of the impact on his health caused by the move, and he gave Clara less money in July and August because of his high hospital bills but gave her whatever he could. Later in September, Jakob Altenberg gave Clara the full 30 RMs. Clara referred to Jakob as a real "mensch."[31]

Elsa also sent Clara three photos. One was a photo with Elsa; her father, Theodore; Anna and Julius Singer; and another man. Clara showed Jakob Altenberg the picture with Julius Singer, Jakob Altenberg's best friend, and seeing it really cheered him up. So, who was the man that Clara didn't know? Could it have been a "certain Pepi Adler," whom Elsa said she had met a few months earlier? Yes!

In early July, the U.S. consulate in Vienna closed. Later that month Clara told Elsa that all emigration had been put on hold and one couldn't get a visa unless he or she had already purchased a ship ticket; and even if someone had the money, without the right connections, purchasing a ship ticket was virtually impossible.

Then, in her inimitable, understated and "rose-colored-glasses" way of presenting things, Clara told Elsa the terrible news: In her letter of August 28 she said, "I want to let you know that yesterday, the 27th, I had to clean out the apartment."

With that massive understatement, Clara was letting Elsa know about her forced relocation from her Hütteldorfer Straße 117 apartment – where she had

---

31   A Yiddish term for a person of integrity and honor.

lived for 28 years – and from the Breitensee neighborhood – where she had lived for 31 years – to a single room, which she now shared with one other person, in a collection apartment in the 2nd District at Konradgasse 1, 3rd floor, door 17. Given how often Clara had told Elsa how happy she was to stay in her apartment, this was one of the worst things that could have happened to her.

With this move, the die had been cast. It was like the movement of tectonic plates. Everything had suddenly changed. The world as Clara knew it had just shifted under her feet. Clara, as well as other Viennese Jews, had been forced to move to districts in Vienna where they were being staged for the mass deportations that began six weeks later. The unexpected upside, if there was one, was that Clara's collection apartment was on the third floor of the same building where her sister Rosalie lived with her husband and son, in an apartment on the first floor.

Clara told Elsa about all the running around she had had to do that day. She had gone to the police station to register her relocation and do the other things necessary for the move. With all the expertise of someone who had moved exactly once in 28 years, Clara's casual remark to Elsa was, "It is always this way with relocations."

As she was leaving, all her friends and acquaintances from Hütteldorfer Straße 117 and from the Breitensee neighborhood came to see her off. "All my friends … wished me good luck… [and] cried when they heard that I had to move out so suddenly …" Clara told Elsa, "I have done good for every person and will continue to do so."

Clara apologized to Elsa if her letter was difficult to read because her hand was shaking so much. The combination of the stress of the urgent running around and the effect of leaving her neighborhood and the many friends she had known over the years had clearly worn her out. And as if the move from her own apartment to a collection apartment wouldn't have been stressful enough, Clara now had to share her one room with a younger woman, a stranger, Fräulein Fanny Steiner.

Clara also apologized to Elsa for her forced relocation – as if she had had any choice in the matter! She said she was getting accustomed to her new living arrangement. It was pointless to be angry.

Here are Clara's own words as she describes the events of August 27.

"My dearly beloved only child!

I want to let you know that yesterday, the 27th, I had to clean out the apartment. All Jews who lived in the outer districts, had to move out and into districts

2, 9 and 20. Now I am living at 2 Bezirk, Konradgasse 1, 3 Stk, Th 17, in the same house where Tante Sali is. It was made available to me. It is a large, airy room with a young woman. The room is partitioned off. The young woman is at work. I am paying rent of 7½ RM per month, including the use of the kitchen ... I was at the police station at Hickelgasse. I had to give notice of departure from my current address and report my new address and had to give notice of departure from my current address at [an office on] Linzerstrasse, from the places where I most recently shopped. Every place, I had to wait a long time. I had a lot of running around. Thank God it's behind me. It's always this way with a relocation.

I had to sell various pieces of furniture, since here I don't have so much room. But one must get used to everything. One can't do anything else. The dear God should only keep me healthy. That is the main thing. I am already aspiring to it ... All my friends already cried when they heard that I had to move out so suddenly. But God is everywhere! ...

Don't make yourself sick over me. Dear God will bring us both together. One just has to hold out. I believe, for you my dear child and for your mother, it has gone best for you and for me. We will soon be together. Have a good time and don't fuss over anything. Just like your mother because one can't change anything. Be thankful for Tante and Onkel Singer. They should stay healthy with their children....

Today I had to register with the police at the former Kaiser Josef Straße. The dear God should continue to give me health and happiness. With every misfortune, somewhere there is a bit of happiness. As I was moving out, all the house dwellers wished me good luck. As well as all my friends from Breitensee. I have only done good for every person. And will continue to do so....

Already last year, I understood that I will have to move. But they let me live here longer ... But God is everywhere. Just keep your head high. This is a very healthy airy room. I should continue to stay healthy, that is the main thing ...

Please excuse my bad handwriting, since my hands are shaking a bit, but hopefully it is readable ...

So, I don't know any more to write today – next time more. With God's help, better news than what is in this letter.

Stay very healthy for me. I greet you and kiss you many thousand times. Your, eternally loving you, mother.

Bye, my little pearl.

Soon your birthday arrives. The 12th of next month. I congratulate you. You should be healthy and live long. Amen!"

With her move to the shared collection apartment, Clara's residence was no longer the central meeting place for Bader family relatives and friends. Rosalie Spielmann's apartment became the new meeting place. Clara went to see Rosalie daily and spent the High Holidays with her. The other family members also came over to Rosalie's apartment to observe the High Holidays: Anna Spitz and her brothers, Max and David Sokal, on the first day of Rosh Hashanah; and Benno, Pepi and Pauli Spielmann, Emma and Kurtl Löff and Helene Diamand on the second day. Dolfi Löff was not there because he was still on his forced-labor assignment.

As it turned out, Clara's roommate, Fanny Steiner, had relatives who were known to Tante Anna and Father. Clara told Elsa that her room was light and airy, and things were much quieter than where she used to live. And in another Clara-shocker, she told Elsa that she had known that this move was coming months earlier and had been preparing for it. Clara had probably seen this coming in June but, as with many other emotionally disturbing situations, she thought it would be less painful to Elsa if she hid the truth.

Clara also told Elsa that she had gone with Fanny Steiner to visit Fanny's oldest brother at the old-age home at Kleine Pfarrgasse, which previously had been the elementary school where, "a long time ago," Clara had gone to school. Clara found out from Fanny that her 74-year-old uncle, Ignatz Heller, was at the old-age home in the 20th District. Ignatz sent regards to Father and to Tante Anna. Clara recalled attending Ignatz's wedding with Fanny's mother, probably when Clara had been married to Theodore Nichtern.

A few weeks later, Clara obtained a letter that had been sent by Tante Anna Singer from New York City to the person who had previously lived in the apartment now occupied by Clara. The name of this woman was never given, possibly because Clara didn't want to reveal it to the Nazi censors.

This woman, who had been an artist in her previous professional life, had been relocated to another collection apartment in the 2nd District at Glockengasse 13 and then deported to the *General Gouvernement* in Poland. Even while dealing with all the stress and difficulties of the relocation, in one of her many acts of kindness, Clara collected other letters sent to this woman and delivered them to the woman's relatives, a family with the name of Kiraly, who lived in the 2nd District at Schmelzgasse 9. The Kiralys said that they would send all the letters to the woman who had been deported. Clara also obtained the woman's address and sent it to Tante Anna.

Later, Clara and Fanny had to move to a different room with another woman, making three people in the same room. Responding to Elsa's reaction to this move, Clara said, "You ask me how I feel about my new place. One must be satisfied because one can't help it." The room where Clara and Fanny had previously lived was taken over by a married couple. The husband worked at the IKG as a carpenter, a "privileged position," which was the reason the couple got a room to themselves.

Clara also mentioned a man and woman who lived in the collection apartment, and who were very musically inclined. The woman played the piano, and the man played the violin. The man had held a significant supervisory position at the building council of Vienna. Clara said that at one time they had been wealthy and that they had musical educations. She said they played beautifully together. We don't know if this is the same couple that displaced Clara from the first room that she had occupied with Fanny Steiner, or a different couple.

In September, Clara found out from Frau Altenberg that the Altenbergs were familiar with a Pepi Adler, who had lived in the 10th District. He and his family had regularly frequented a coffee house located in the neighborhood where the Altenbergs had lived before they were relocated to the 13th District. Clara found out from Frau Altenberg that Pepi Adler had worked in an iron foundry. "You write that for the past three months you have gotten to know a certain Mr. Pepi Adler … I am very happy. My dear child, I pray daily for you … What does Father say about it?… Is he [Pepi] good to you? I hope so. He doesn't need to please me, only you."

Also in September, all Jews in the Reich and its territories, who were six years or older, were ordered to wear a yellow Star of David on their outer clothing. This was the ultimate humiliation for the Jewish population and facilitated the identification and separation of the Jewish population from the rest of the Viennese population, clearly identifying them as pariahs. The fact that Clara never mentioned this in any of her letters to Elsa was astonishing. Even with her world caving in around her, Clara would do everything she could to avoid delivering bad news to Elsa.

October marked the restart of the mass deportations to the East and the total prohibition of emigration from the Reich. In her letter of October 15, after 3½ years of constantly worsening conditions and increased Nazi persecution, Clara finally acknowledged the terrible situation for Jews in Vienna. She said that the transports to Poland had started again. At 3 p.m. on Tuesday, October 14, a transport had left for Poland. Clara said that a Herr und Frau Willig, who were the main renters of the collection apartment where she was living, would be deported to Poland on October 28, and a man in another room would be deported on October 19. Then Clara finally came out and said – "It is a tragic drama here."

Those few words made up the only negative comment that Clara made about the deportations. Either because she didn't want to upset Elsa or because of the Nazi censorship, she never mentioned the deportations again, and she never mentioned the wearing of the yellow star, which was an anathema to the Jews.

Clara ended her letter of October 15 with a simple *"Servus Schnukerl,"* – Bye, Darling! This was a very minimalistic closing compared to previous letters, which were progressively more emotional, and where only a month earlier she had closed with the words *"Your eternally loving you mother."*

Even though Clara said very little about the deportations restarting, it was quite clear that the situation affected her greatly. I suspect that with everything that had happened during the course of 1941, Clara recognized that all hope of getting out of Vienna had ended and understood that it would just be a matter of time before she also would be deported. And yet it seemed that she was still trying to downplay it to Elsa to the extent possible and to make it seem as if it was just another day at the office.

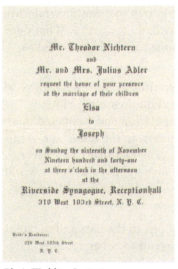

Elsa's Wedding Invitation

In November, Elsa received Carl Spitz's second letter, sent in response to Elsa's wedding invitation.

Carl told Elsa that starting in August, he had been employed as an elevator operator at the headquarters of the Bank of America in San Francisco; he had a steady job and would become a member of the union. He was earning $125 a month, up from his previous salary of $75 a month. He now had enough money for his needs and could send some money to Vienna. He said it was impossible to send packages home, so he sent money, and even that was iffy. Otto, who was living in Brussels with his wife, Cilli, was in bad shape and needed money to buy enough food. He said that Otto was keeping things together despite everything.

Carl said he was receiving letters from his mother and his uncle Max Sokal describing how really bad things were in Vienna. The family members wrote what they could get through the censors. Carl said that he and his sister, Grete, sent photos, which helped keep their mother's spirits up. He also said that he was glad that Clara visited his mother often.

Carl passed along news from Grete, who was still working as a domestic in England. Carl told Elsa about a new meeting place for Austrian refugees in England established by The Austrian Centre. The Austrian Centre, which was originally established in 1939, helped to serve the cultural, social and political needs of the displaced Austrian refugees such as Grete.

Grete mentioned the Austrian Centre's facility in the Swiss Cottage neighborhood of London, a location that included a theater that performed plays and had other entertainment to try to create a link to the life the refugees had left behind. Grete also had told him the work situation for refugees had improved now that the internments were basically over, and that Grete had heard from Mali.

Carl said he tried to avoid despair "in these terrible times" and said he wished that he had resisted more in the beginning. Now he and others did whatever they could, no matter how small – he said that "As long as there lives an antifascist, I will fight against the bandits who want to make life a living hell."

Carl closed by wishing Elsa and her future husband his best. His wife, Felicia, and his sister-in-law Jenna added their best wishes also.

The mail from the U.S. had been taking several weeks to get to Vienna. In a letter from Elsa received in early November, Clara learned that Elsa was engaged and would be married on November 16. With this date in mind, Clara prepared as best she could to celebrate Elsa's wedding from 4,200 miles away in Nazi-occupied Vienna.

In Clara's last letter, dated November 17, she told Elsa how three days earlier she had gone to the cemetery to invite all the deceased relatives to be at Elsa's marriage in spirit. She wrote, "Friday morning, I was at the cemetery. I invited all my dear and beloved so that they should be in spirit under the wedding canopy. The golden grandparents together with Uncle Bernhard. All should bring happiness and luck forever." The next day she went to the old age home on Malzgasse and picked up some baked goods for the gathering of family and friends that they were going to have over to celebrate Elsa's wedding.

Then on Sunday, November 16, the day of the wedding, the pianist who lived with her husband and Clara in the collection apartment played the Wedding March from "Lohengrin" in celebration of Elsa's wedding day. Then the couple played together, with the woman on the piano and the man on the violin. Clara said it was beautiful and changed the mood of the entire Konradgasse 1 collection apartment building. Clara thanked God that she had lived long enough to know that her daughter was getting married.

Clara told Elsa that all the family "would very much have liked to have been there [for Elsa's wedding], but it was not in our destiny." Clara went to Tante Spitz's place where, together with David and Max Sokal, Helene Diamand, and Emma and Kurtl Löff, she celebrated Elsa's wedding "in spirit."

They managed to have some cake and drinks. Clara said that they sang the Jewish wedding celebration dance song *"Chosen Kallah Mazeltov"* (congratulations to the bride and groom). Clara said that Rolf Nichtern and the Spielmanns sent their best wishes to the bride and groom and said that Dolfi Löff was not able to be there because he was still working in Wohnlager Mitterweißenbach.[32] Dolfi sent "heartfelt congratulations" and kisses to Elsa for her wedding. Clara recalled how much fun Dolfi was and that he would have entertained everyone. She said that she had written to Leon and Maxl about Elsa's wedding but hadn't heard back from them.

Amid all this, Clara asked if Elsa had written to Mali and asked Elsa to send Dolfi a letter at his address: A. Löff; Wohnlager Mitterweißenbach; Post Ischl; Ober-Donau.

Clara reminisced about the November 16 date, saying that she was married on the 16th of January and that she thought that Maxl's birthday was on the 16th also. So, 16 was a fortuitous date. Clara told Elsa that she should bet on number 16 in the lottery.

Clara said that the collection apartment co-dwellers sent Elsa their best wishes and that Clara would convey Elsa's wishes to all the relatives and acquaintances. Clara sent congratulations to Pepi Adler's parents "from the depths of my heart" and wished the same future wedding experience for the children of Anna and Julius Singer.

In her last letter to Elsa, Clara said, "I thank the dear God that he has let me live [long enough] to know that you are married."

Clara's last letter ended with "Uncountable Kisses."

What a moving picture is created by these accounts of Clara and other family members and friends vicariously celebrating Elsa's wedding! Despite the upheaval in her life, Clara seemed determined to be upbeat and positive and revel in this happy time for her daughter – and to focus on the positive for Elsa's sake. But her words thanking God that she had "lived long enough" to know that her daughter was getting married may show that she understood that her very survival was precarious at that point. It would otherwise be an odd comment from

---

32   Wohnlager Mitterweißenbach was a forced labor camp that predominantly was for Viennese Jews, sent there to work on road-construction projects, from June 1940 to September 1942, after which they were deported. Source: Zeitgeschichte Museum Ebensee.

a woman who was only 59 years old at the time. And, of course, she didn't know that this would be her last letter to her daughter.

Elsa's Wedding Photo

The November 30 letter from Elsa to Clara is the only letter that exists written by Elsa to Clara. This letter was returned to Elsa in July 1942. Elsa by then had been married for eight months and was living with Pepi and her in-laws at 2288 Mott Ave. Apt. 4D, Far Rockaway, NY.

In the letter Elsa wrote that she had been married for 14 days and that 50 people had been at the wedding: almost all the U.S. relatives, the Schorrs and Manns from Ottakringerstraße, and Trude Markstein and her husband; but Ernestine and Felix Atlas had not been there. Elsa said the wedding was very nice. Her father beamed with pride.

Elsa said that she didn't cry and held herself together. She said that Tante Anna was very good to her and had worked hard cooking and baking for the wedding reception.

Elsa said that her husband was very good and thoughtful. She said that she was sending Clara a photo, which was all she could send from her wedding and hoped it would get through. Elsa wrote about how much she would have liked Clara to have been at the wedding with her.

My mother wrote to my grandmother, "We have a beautiful apartment. We live with the [Adler] parents. You will see everything when you come here, which with God's help, will be soon. Just try to stay healthy, to get through these times."

My mother's final words were "Send all the relatives and friends many greetings and kisses and many, many kisses for you."

The letter simply ends with "Your Elsa."

I found this letter in the packet along with all the letters from my grandmother and other relatives. It must have been heartbreaking for my mother to have this letter returned after so many months and to realize that her mother had not even seen the wedding picture she had sent – especially since Clara's letters had stopped so abruptly after the one celebrating Elsa's marriage. And what Elsa did not know was that her mother had already been deported on June 9 and murdered at Maly Trostinec on June 15, a few weeks before the date that this letter was returned.

Part II: Now - Finding "Sweet Little Pauli"

THE LAST SURVIVOR

As I look back on my journey to find my surviving relatives, I can see it now as a series of discoveries, with each discovery leading to a number of serendipitous events.

The first discovery came from our meeting with Dr. Elisabeth Klamper on August 9, 2010, when I learned where and when my grandmother was murdered. I came out of that meeting so removed from the comfort zone of what I thought I knew that I was driven to find out more about my grandmother and what had happened to her. Then there was the second discovery – the packet of letters. I have already discussed both of these in the prologue to this book.

Once I had the letters, I needed to get them translated. This led to discovering the names of relatives I had never heard of and trying to learn more about them.

But before I go into details about my journey to find surviving relatives, I need to return to the time during and shortly after the first translations of the letters were completed.

Translations and Names

When I looked at the handwriting in the letters, I was quickly struck by the fact that some of the letters were written in a penmanship style similar to what you would typically see today, and some were written in a very ornate penmanship style where, at least for me, it was nearly impossible to make out the individual letters, let alone read the words. That everyday penmanship is known as *Lateinschrift* and it looks very much like how we write today. The penmanship that is basically unreadable to someone not schooled in this version of cursive is known as *Kurrentschrift*. It is the very flowery penmanship related to different variations of German gothic lettering.

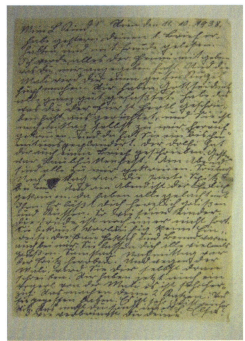

"My Dearest Child"
October 11, 1938
Letter written in Kurrentschrift

"My Dearest Only Beloved Child"
September 25, 1941
Letter written in Lateinschrift

It was possible to divide the letters into two groups by penmanship style: The first group consisted of letters written from September 20, 1938, to May 27, 1940. They were written in *Kurrentschrift*. The second group were those letters written from June 11, 1940, to November 30, 1941, as well as a few other letters written in *Lateinschrift*.

Because the *Lateinschrift* letters were relatively straightforward to read, in 2011 we were able to find a translator in Fort Wayne, Joy Gieschen. Joy had an undergraduate degree in German and had recently returned from Austria, where she had been teaching English to Austrian high school students. Eventually, with the help of a relative living in New York, my cousin Julie Metz, I was able to make contact with Michael Simonson of the Leo Baeck Institute in New York City. Michael connected me with Marianne Salinger, a volunteer and Holocaust survivor from Germany, who was able to provide me with an initial translation of the *Kurrentschrift* letters. This was completed by July 2014.

As luck would have it, at the time that Joy was doing the translations of the letters written in *Lateinschrift*, she was in the midst of pursuing a master's degree in education from Indiana University Purdue University Fort Wayne (now Purdue University Fort Wayne). One day Joy, who was the first to discover the different names in the letters and to recognize the two different penmanship styles, asked if she could use the long-distance dialogue between my grandmother and my mother contained in the letters as a basis for her master's project, to which I enthusiastically agreed. This led to a recognition that to better understand what my grandmother was trying to express and the conditions under which my grandmother and mother had been living before and after my mother's emigration from Vienna, we needed to take a trip to Vienna.

Vienna 2012

In order to prepare for the trip to Vienna, in April 2012 Fran, Joy and I met with Dr. Ann Millin and Ms. Theresa Pollin, two researchers at the United States Holocaust Memorial Museum (USHMM). The most important takeaway from that meeting was the suggestion that we meet Elizabeth (Betsy) Anthony (now Dr. Anthony), who was a former employee of the USHMM, was living in Vienna with her Viennese husband and, at that time, was pursuing a PhD in history from Clark University, which she received in May of 2016.

Then in June 2012, Fran, Joy and I traveled to Vienna. The trip led to four important outcomes: (1) We met and reviewed our findings with Elisabeth Klamper, with whom I had been corresponding by email since we first met in August 2010; (2) we went to the IKG and found more family records; (3) we met Betsy Anthony for the first time; and (4), we discovered the Stones of Remembrance,[33] the Viennese version of Germany's *Stolpersteine*.

---

[33]   The Stones of Remembrance were fashioned after the *Stolpersteine* program that was started in Germany in 1992. *Stolpersteine* (stumbling stones) were typically placed in front of a Holocaust victim's last known residence prior to deportation. In Germany, a *Stolperstein* consists of an approximately 4-inch square brass plaque enclosed in a paving block known as a sett or Belgium block; whereas in Vienna, the brass plaque is about an 8-inch square and is typically placed directly into the sidewalk in front of the last known residence of the Holocaust victim.

As we were walking along the streets of the 2nd District of Vienna, Leopold-stadt, from where most of the Jews, including my grandmother, were deported during the mass deportations of 1941 and 1942, we noticed that the Stones of Remembrance went from one location to another, many times close to one another. Each Stone of Remembrance represented the last known residence of the person who was deported from that location and had that person's name. This resulted in a trail of connected "Stones" that wandered through the district, forming the Path of Remembrance.

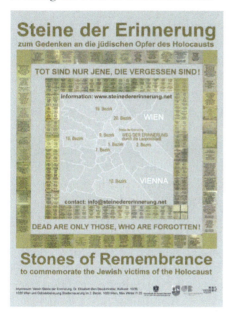

Steine der Erinnerung Poster
(Used with permission from the Association of the Stones of Remembrance)

When we got back from this trip, we knew that more work was needed to refine the names and information from the *Lateinschrift* letters that Joy had translated and had used for her master's project. I also continued to maintain contact with Betsy Anthony. In 2013, I knew that she had returned to Washington, D.C., and had assumed a position at the USHMM as a staff scholar at the Mandel Center for Advanced Holocaust Studies, specializing in research on the use of the International Tracing Service (ITS) digital archive.[34]

I also contacted Dr. Elisabeth Ben David-Hindler, the person responsible for the Stones of Remembrance project, with the intention to dedicate a Stone of Remembrance for my grandmother. And I initiated a project at the Leo Baeck Institute to get the *Kurrentschrift* letters translated. A few years later, with the help of another Fort Wayne resident and now family friend, Carol Jackson, all the letters were transcribed and then translated once more, resulting in an improved set of translated letters that were used to uncover the individual stories given in Part I.

---

34   The International Tracing Service, ITS, was established in 1943 by the British Red Cross as it became clear that the Allies would win World War II and that it would be necessary to find survivors once the War in Europe ended. In 2019, the ITS changed its name to the Arolsen Archives and is working diligently to make its contents accessible and available to the public. The archives contain the names of Holocaust victims and survivors in a variety of documents, including name cards, transport lists, concentration camp records, victim search requests and photos of objects belonging to victims.

Who Survived?

Now fast-forward to April 2014. I made arrangements with Dr. Elisabeth Ben David-Hindler to dedicate a Stone of Remembrance for my grandmother, Clara, at her last known place of residence, the now reconstructed building in the 2nd District located at the corner of Taborstraße and Konradgasse, where her collection apartment was located and where she lived until her deportation to Maly Trostinec on June 9, 1942.

The date for the Stone of Remembrance dedication was May 18, 2014. As I was preparing for this trip, I continued to do research on life in Vienna under Nazi occupation and had correspondence with Betsy Anthony to see if she could research the ITS digital archive to find information about the family members that I had discovered. With this in mind, I decided that it would be worthwhile to take a trip to Washington to meet with Betsy once again. I also decided to include a trip to New York City to meet Dr. Edith Kurzweil, with whom I was put in contact through Michael Simonson of the Leo Baeck Institute.

As a result of my research on life in Vienna under Nazi occupation, I had discovered a book written by Dr. Edith Kurzweil. Dr. Kurzweil was a Holocaust survivor, a prominent New York intellectual and a recipient of the National Humanities Medal in 2003. Her 2004 book, *Nazi Laws and Jewish Lives – Letters from Vienna*, was based on letters sent to her from Viennese relatives living under Nazi occupation, especially her grandmother. After having read Dr. Kurzweil's book, I thought that meeting her might help me write a story based on my grandmother's letters. Dr. Kurzweil's book linked the letters written by her relatives to the Nazi laws issued and promulgated during a time period that overlapped the time period of my grandmother's letters. Because of this, I thought it would be important to speak with her, and I made arrangements to visit Dr. Kurzweil in New York City before our trip to Washington, D.C.

On April 15, 2014, Fran and I flew to New York to meet Dr. Kurzweil. We met her mid-morning of the next day at her apartment on 64th Street, just a few hundred feet down the block from Lincoln Center. As I recall, Dr. Kurzweil had a beautiful apartment filled with antique furniture, books and memorabilia and, from her 16th floor window, a clearly visible view of the fountain in front of Lincoln Center's Metropolitan Opera House.

Meeting Dr. Kurzweil was a unique experience. We talked for a while and then we went out to lunch at a nearby restaurant, Le Pain Quotidien, where we talked some more.

Although she was 88 and a bit frail, her mind was very sharp. She identified references that I should review to understand what life was like for the Jews of Vienna from 1938 to 1945. My main questions to her were related to how to write a book about my grandmother's letters. Her answer was "you write around it," which has taken me a few years to do.

Later that afternoon, we boarded a train to Washington D.C. to meet with Betsy Anthony, whom we saw the next morning.

As I was doing my research on the letters, the family names that came up most frequently were members of the Bader and Spielmann families. For the Baders, it was Mali, Leon and their son, Maxl; and for the Spielmanns, it was Benno, Max and "sweet little Pauli," who had been identified many times in the letters and who I originally thought was the son of Max Spielmann. In addition, my mother had a collection of personal address books from 1950 to 1980. Periodically, I would go through these books and would find names that corresponded to the names in the letters. Max Spielmann's name appeared the most frequently in these books. He had been living in Sydney, Australia, at least through the mid-1980s.

A few weeks before meeting Betsy at the USHMM, I had a series of e-mail exchanges with her. I gave Betsy what information I thought I knew about Mali, Leon, Maxl, Benno, Max and Pauli. At this point I knew that Mali had been interned on the Isle of Man and that she had survived. I had no idea about what had happened to Leon and Maxl Bader. I knew that Max Spielmann had survived, but I didn't know what had happened to Paul Spielmann. Since we knew the most about Max and Paul Spielmann, we focused on them. I gave Betsy the last known address that I had for Max from my mother's 1980s address book.

ITS Card for Max Spielmann
Source: ITS (Arolsen) Archives

ITS Card for Paul Spielmann
Source: ITS (Arolsen) Archives

Using the information that I provided, Betsy did an extensive search of the ITS records for Max and Paul Spielmann. She discovered details of their terrible journey through the camps, but most importantly that Paul had survived the camps and made it to Israel (Palestine at that time). In 1945, Paul emigrated to Israel; and in 1946 Max Spielmann emigrated to Australia and was alive at least through 1980. Betsy also found out that Leon and Maxl had been victims of the Holocaust.

Shortly thereafter, as I was examining the Yad Vashem victims and survivors database, I came across a 1999 Page of Testimony from a Shaul Spielmann. Shaul gave the names of Josefine and Benno Spielmann as his parents. In the process of reexamining the translated letters, I recognized that Paul's parents were Josefine and Benno, as I had seen their names together many times in the letters. But who was Shaul? Was he Paul? If so, then I knew he was still alive as of 1999.

Shaul Spielmann's Page of Testimony
Source: Yad Vashem

May 18, 2014

The plan was to take a May 2014 trip to Vienna with Fran. The trip was to be an opportunity to do some more research, to dedicate a Stone of Remembrance for my grandmother, Clara, and to take a few days for some Vienna sightseeing.

Unfortunately, the trip didn't go as planned. Fran was not able to travel to Vienna with me. Her daughter, Lisa, who lives in Rochester, N.Y., and was visiting Fort Wayne with her family to attend a family event, had been hospitalized a week or so earlier, had had two surgeries and had been in and out of the hospital's intensive care unit. Fran had to stay home. So, I traveled alone to Vienna for the Stone of Remembrance Ceremony.

The good news was that Lisa recovered and basically has been in good health.

Sunday, May 18, 2014, was a cold and damp day in Vienna. It had rained all morning. There were about 100 people in their raincoats gathered together at the dedication opening ceremonies, standing and sitting with umbrellas. They had come from all over the world: The United States, South Africa, South America, Australia, Canada, Israel and several countries in Europe.

Stones of Remembrance Ceremony – May 18, 2014

The ceremony began at 10 a.m. After about an hour of introductory speeches, we spent a good part of the next six hours walking through the streets of Leopoldstadt, making stops at each location where a Stone of Remembrance was to be dedicated.

At one of those stops, a Mr. Gershon Günsberger, from Australia, dedicated a Stone of Remembrance for his uncle. A little later, I dedicated the Stone of Remembrance for my grandmother.

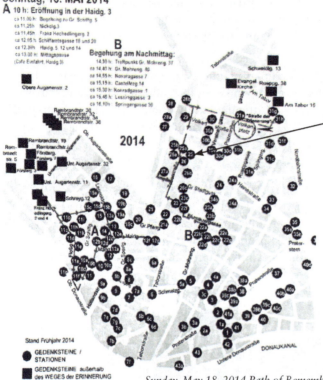

WEG DER ERINNERUNG durch die LEOPOLDSTADT
Sonntag, 18. MAI 2014

CHAJE
NICHTERN
GEB. BADER
20.3.1882

AM 9.6.1942
NACH MALY TROSTINEC
DEPORTIERT
AM 15.6.1942
ERMORDET

*Stone of Remembrance
for Clara (with her Hebrew
name, Chaje)*

*Sunday, May 18, 2014 Path of Remembrance
(Used with permission from the Association of the Stones
of Remembrance)*

*Irv dedicating Stone
of Remembrance
for his grandmother,
Clara.*

Shortly after my dedication, there was a break in the action, and we were milling about on a street corner. Since I was aware that Gershon was Australian, I asked him if he might know how I could get information about Max Spielmann, who, as of the mid-1980s, had been living in Australia. I also told Gershon that I thought that Max was no longer alive and that the last known address I had for Max was Victoria Place, 168 Bellevue Hill, Sydney, Australia. Gershon turned to me and said that he knew exactly where Max had lived. It was only a few blocks from where Gershon was then living. I was in shock. Then came the immediate aftershock.

While we were standing on a damp street corner in Leopoldstadt, waiting for the Stone of Remembrance Ceremonies to resume, Gershon pulled out his iPhone and dialed up the link to the Sydney *Chevrah Kadisha*, the Jewish burial society. Within a few minutes after making that connection, he showed me a photograph of Max Spielmann's headstone and gave me the name and contact information for the cemetery where Max Spielmann was buried.

The headstone was very revealing. I discovered that Max had died in 1992. I also discovered that Max's wife's name was Lilly and that she had died in 1998 and that they appeared to have had no children, but they had a nephew and two nieces.

Gravestone of Max and Lilly Spielmann at Rookwood Cemetery, Sydney, Australia

Is Anyone Still Alive?

So, this is where I was on May 18, 2014. I knew that Max Spielmann had died in 1992. I knew that there were some relatives related to him by marriage. I didn't know if they were alive. I knew there was a person named Shaul Spielmann who had been living in Israel and was alive in 1999. And it appeared likely that Shaul was Paul, but I wasn't sure.

A week or so later, having returned to Fort Wayne and recovered from jet lag, I contacted the cemetery in Sydney to find out if Max and Lilly Spielmann had any living relatives and, if so, would the cemetery contact them on my behalf and let me know if I could contact them directly. Because of the 14-hour time difference between Fort Wayne, Indiana, and Sydney, Australia, it took a few days before this was all sorted out.

Eventually, I was put in touch with the two nieces of Max and Lilly Spielmann, Evelyn and Robbie Bowmer. This being the age of scamming, malware and identity theft, the Bowmers were very reluctant to tell me very much about Max Spielmann. So, after another e-mail exchange in which I told the Bowmers that Max Spielmann was my mother's cousin and that I was trying to find relatives on the Bader side of my family, they told me that as of 2006, Paul was alive and was living in Israel; but that, unfortunately, they had lost touch with him. Evelyn and Robbie told me that Paul had a son, whose name was Benny. He was married, and his wife's name was Katie. Benny had come to the United States in 2002 and, at least through 2006, was living in Huntington Woods, Michigan, three hours by car from our home in Fort Wayne, Indiana. Another shocker! What to do next?

Meeting "Sweet Little Pauli" – The End of the Journey

My next step was to see if I could find a Benny Spielmann living in or around Detroit; and if so, could I make contact with him. So – not knowing what else to do – I went to Google and did a search for "Benny Spielmann and Detroit."

I got four hits with four different telephone numbers. I called the four numbers, with no answer for the first three. When I called the fourth number, a woman answered, who I later found out was Benny's mother-in-law, Hannah Moss. I told the woman that I was a relative of Benny Spielmann and that I was trying to get in touch with him. I was sure she thought I was scamming her. After I gave her more information about myself, my connection to Benny and what I was trying to do, she was sort of convinced that I knew something about the Spielmanns. She told me that she would take my number and ask Benny to call me. Then, two days later, Benny tried to call me and left a voice message. The next day I called him back. He answered the phone. I told him who I was and what I was doing. There was complete silence. It was as if Benny had gone into a state of shock! I had just hit him in the head with an imaginary baseball bat. After a long pause, we started to talk.

I told Benny how I was related to him and how I had traced and found him. He told me that the only living relatives of whom he had been aware were his immediate family members. Benny told me that his father, Paul, now Shaul, was alive and living in Israel.

I had found "Sweet Pauli," and he was alive!

So, after all these shocks, could there be another one? Yes! It was what I like to call the Big **WOW!**

Benny told me that not only was his father alive and well, but that his father, his mother, his sister and her family were going to be at his house in about three weeks, the week of July 7.

Then on Saturday, July 12, 2014, Fran and I drove to Huntington Woods for a meeting with my then-83-year-old cousin, who I had not known was alive a month earlier, and who had not known that he had any other family in the world, other than his immediate family.

Irv with Shaul at their first meeting on July 12, 2014.

Needless to say, the meeting was incredibly emotional for everyone.

Fran and I spent all afternoon, that evening and the following morning with the Spielmann family: Shaul and his wife, Miriam; Benny and his wife, Katie, and their children; Einat and her husband, Naor, and their children; and Benny's in-laws, Gordon and Hannah Moss.

Shaul told me that when he first arrived in Israel in 1945, the authorities in Israel had changed his name from Paul to Shaul. He told me that he had been involved in every major Israeli conflict, as Israel fought to preserve its statehood. He told me that he now lives in Ashkelon, about 23 kms north of Gaza, with his wife, Miriam, and has led an interesting and fulfilling life; but until I contacted his son Benny, the only other relatives that he knew had survived the Holocaust were his grandfather, Israel Spielmann, who died in 1952, and his uncle, Max Spielmann, who died in 1992 – and after Shaul entered the camps, he had never seen either of them again. As far as he knew, he had no other living relatives with ties to his Viennese roots.

I told Shaul about the letters and how by reading the letters, I had discovered the Spielmanns. I told him how the ITS searches that I did with Betsy Anthony helped me eventually find him.

As a result of my mother's collection of letters, I found a side of my family that I never knew existed, and whom my mother was emotionally unable to speak about – the Bader side; and that included my cousin, Shaul Spielmann, the last living family member who had survived the horrors of the Holocaust.

Epilogue: The Families And Friends - And What Happened To Them

THE BADER AND THE NICHTERN FAMILIES

In the late 1800s, some of my Bader ancestors left the Galician city of Lemberg (now Lwow/Lviv, Ukraine) and some of my Nichtern ancestors left the Galician city of Tarnow (now Tarnow, Poland) and moved to Vienna. Both of these families participated in the great migration of Jews from their ancestral cities and towns in the eastern part of the Austrian-Hungarian Empire to Western Europe. Both of these families, steeped in Orthodox Judaism, made the trek from their ancestral Jewish homes in Lemberg and Tarnow to find a better life in Vienna, which also was more secular.

I have identified families and family members who are tied directly to the letters and who are my relatives on the Bader side of my family. The names, dates and relationships are a result of several years of researching archival materials and databases that are identified in Appendix L of this book.

I will begin by describing how the various Bader and Nichtern family members relate to one another through the genealogical charts shown on the next two pages. The person who connects both genealogical charts is my mother, Elsa. Her mother was Clara Nichtern, born Bader. Her father was Theodore Nichtern.

Here is what I know as of this writing about the family members and very close friends before and during the Nazi occupation of Vienna and the Holocaust, and in some cases, what happened to them.

Genealogy- Bader Side:

Holocaust victims in red

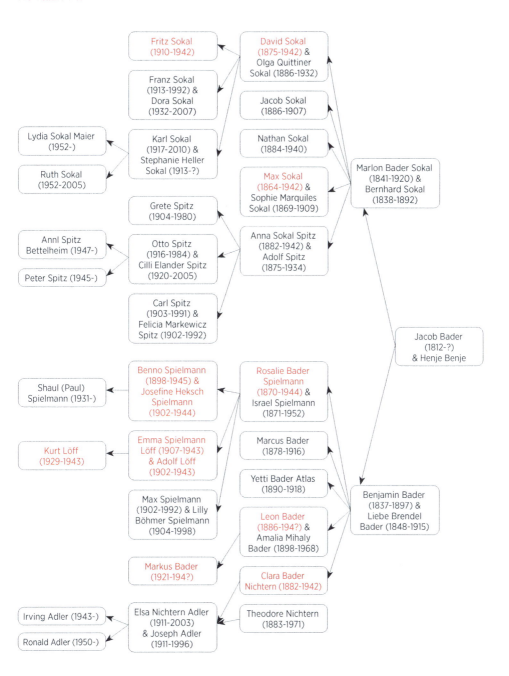

Genealogy- Nichtern Side:

Holocaust victims in red

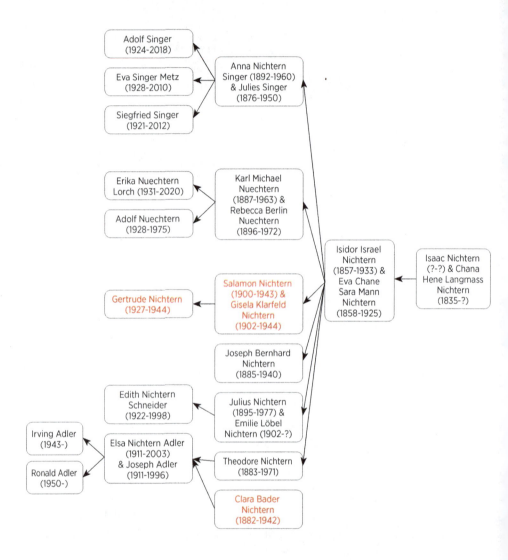

The Baders

The Baders who left Lemberg and went to Vienna, Austria, were Benjamin and his wife, Liebe; his sister Marion and her husband, Bernhard (Berl) Sokal, and the children who were born before the move.

Benjamin Bader (1837-1897) and Liebe Brendel Bader (1848-1915) were born in Lemberg, Galicia. They had a religious marriage ceremony on November 16, 1869, in Lemberg; then they had a second, officially recognized marriage ceremony in Vienna on October 19, 1890. They lived in the 2nd District at Leopoldgasse 29.

Marion Bader Sokal (1841-1920) and Bernhard Sokal (1838-1892) were also born in Lemberg. They most likely had a religious marriage in Lemberg and a second, officially recognized marriage in Vienna, Austria.

Based on my research to date, Benjamin and Liebe lived in Vienna with their five children: Rosalie (1870-1944), Marcus (1878-1916), Clara (1882-1942), Leon (1886-194?)[35] and Yetti (1890-1918). Their move was sometime after 1882 but before 1886, since Clara was born in Lemberg while Leon and Yetti were born in Vienna.

Marion and Berl also lived in Vienna with their five children: Max (1864-1942), David (1875-1942), Anna (1882-1942), Nathan (1884-1940) and Jacob (1886-1907). Since Anna was born on March 7, 1882, in Vienna, while Clara was born March 20,1882, in Lemberg, the Sokals must have moved to Vienna earlier than the Baders.

The key relationship between the Baders and the Sokals was the one between Anna and Clara. They were first cousins, and their birthdays were only 13 days apart. It was clear from my grandmother's letters that Clara and Anna had shared a very close emotional bond since childhood.

With regard to the Bader siblings:

- Rosalie Bader married Israel Spielmann in Vienna in 1897. They had three children: Benno, Max and Emma.

- Clara married Theodore Nichtern on January 16, 1910. They had one child, Elsa.

- Yetti married Philip Atlas in 1913. She died in 1918. She had no children with Philip. Philip remarried and had children. The Atlas family remained very close with Clara, presumably because of the tie to Yetti.

---

35   There is no confirmed date-of-death for Leon Bader. The IKG records use May 8, 1945, the official date of the end of WWII in Europe.

- Leon Bader married Amalia (Mali) Mihaly on June 20, 1920. They had one child, Markus (Maxl).

- I know nothing about Marcus Bader. My guess is that Maxl was named after him.

Of the Bader siblings who were alive at the time of the *Anschluss* – Rosalie, Clara and Leon – none survived World War II.

The Nichterns

Isidor Nichtern and Eva Chane Sara Nichtern (born Mann) were married in Tarnow in 1882. They must have immigrated to Vienna shortly thereafter since all their children, starting in 1883 with their oldest child, my grandfather, Theodore, were born in Vienna.

The photo below taken in Vienna ca. 1910 shows the entire Nichtern family.

In the back row: Theodore (1883-1971), Josef Bernhard (1885-1940), Julius (1895-1972), Anna (1892-1980) and Karl Michael (1887-1969); in the front row: Eva Chane Sara (1858-1925), Salamon (1900-1943) and Isidor (1856-1933).

With regard to the Nichtern siblings:

- Theodore Nichtern was married three times. First to Clara Bader in 1910. (They were divorced in 1921). Then to Pauline Markstein-Atlas in 1923. And then again to Olga Stiassny in 1934.

- Josef Bernhard was never married.

- Julius Nichtern married Emilie (Millie) Löbel in 1921. They had one child, Edith.

- Anna Nichtern Singer married Julius Singer in 1920. They had three children, Siegfried (Fritz), Adolf (Dolfi) and Eva.

- Karl Michael Nuechtern married Rebecca Berlin in 1926. They had two children, Adolf and Erika.
- Salamon (Rolf) Nichtern married Gisela Klarfeld in 1925. They had one child, Gertrude.

Of the six Nichtern siblings, four were able to escape from Vienna. Only Salamon and Bernhard were not able to get out. I knew very little about either of them.

Bernhard Nichtern
September 1938

Salamon Nichtern
May 18, 1920

From my grandmother's letters, I learned that Bernhard had a fatal head injury from an accident. My grandmother didn't mention that he died until the following year. Maybe she was aware that Elsa had found this out through her Nichtern relatives in New York. Salamon Nichtern, who worked at the Rothschild hospital where Bernhard died, probably communicated this to his siblings in New York City. Based on additional research, I found out that Bernhard died in October 1940 and was buried in the *Zentralfriedhof* (central cemetery) in Vienna.

Salamon, his wife, Gisela (1902-1944), and their daughter, Gertrude (1927-1944), were sent to Theresienstadt in October 1942. Salamon died in Theresienstadt in 1943, and Gisela and Gertrude died in Auschwitz in 1944.

The four Nichtern siblings who left Vienna made it to the U.S. over the 20 month-period from August 1938 to April 1940.

The first of the Nichtern siblings to escape from Vienna was Karl Nuechtern. Karl and his family left in August 1938 and were able to come to the U.S. with the help of Julius Garfinkle. His wife, Fanny (born Mann), was related to the Nichtern siblings through their mother, Eva Chane Sara Nichtern (born Mann). Fanny's father, Abraham Mann, and Eva Chane Sara were siblings. Julius Garfinkle, who worked in the garment business in New York City, was the person who obtained affidavits for Karl and his siblings.

Theodore and Olga Nichtern left Vienna in early May 1939 on a transit visa that allowed them to stay in England only for a week or so. Then they left for New York City.

Julius Nichtern followed a similar transit visa path as Theodore, leaving Vienna in June 1939, making a short stop in London and then going on to New York City. His wife, Millie, left Vienna in early 1939, since she was able to get work as a domestic in England. Later in 1939, Millie joined Elsa to work at the vicarage. Millie left England and came to New York City in August 1939.

Finally, Anna, Julius and Eva Singer left Vienna in March 1940 and joined her three brothers in New York the following month.

The children of Julius and Millie Nichtern and of Anna and Julius Singer took a different path out of Vienna. Shortly after the *Anschluss*, Edith Nichtern, 16 at the time, and the Singers' two sons - Siegfried (Fritz), who was 17, and Adolf (Dolfi), who was 14 - boarded a train from Vienna and traveled on their own to London. All three lived with the families of relatives who had emigrated from Tarnow to England during the late 1800s. Later, Edith lived with her mother at the vicarage. Then Edith left England and arrived in New York City in September 1939. The two Singer boys remained in England during World War II.

I knew considerably more about the Nichterns than I did about the Baders, since I knew some of them as I was growing up in New York City.

I vaguely recall meeting Anna and Julius Singer and their daughter, Eva, as I was growing up in New York City. They lived in Manhattan's Upper West Side, the same general neighborhood where I spent most of my first nine years before my family moved to Far Rockaway, New York.

Of all the Nichterns/Singers, other than my grandfather, I knew Dolfi the best. Dolfi got married in England in 1945 and then immigrated to the U.S. about 1956. Fritz remained in England. I don't recall ever meeting him. My mother and Dolfi had a very good relationship, and our families would get together a few times during the year, especially at the Passover holiday, when our first Seder was with my father's family and the second Seder was with my mother's family – my New York City Nichtern relatives.

I met my Great Uncle Julius, Great Aunt Millie and my mother's cousin Edith when I moved to Ann Arbor, Michigan, in 1965. I don't recall meeting them before that time. My mother was close to them in Vienna and especially in England when my mother and Millie were working as domestics and living at the vicarage.

I am sure that I met Karl Nuechtern, although I don't have specific memories about him. I recall that in the late 1950s I spoke to Karl's son, Adolf (Adi), about a summer job as a draftsman in Adi's engineering firm, since I was taking technical drawing courses at Brooklyn Technical High School around that time. Karl decided to use the name Nuechtern instead of Nichtern. I have never really understood why, although through genealogy research, I have found other ancestors with the Nuechtern name.

I knew my maternal grandfather, Theodore, very well. I also knew his wife, Olga (the third marriage for both of them), and her daughter from her second marriage, Henrietta (Henny) Spitzer. Theodore and Olga would visit my family regularly, especially at the Jewish holidays.

My grandmother, Clara Bader Nichtern

Wedding Photo of Clara and Theodore

Elsa, Clara and Theodore ca. 1916

On January 16, 1910, Clara Bader married Theodore Nichtern at the Jewish Community Synagogue in the 20th District at Kluckygasse 11.

My mother, Elsa, was born on September 12, 1911. Sometime in 1913 Clara, Theodore and Elsa moved into the apartment in the 13th District (at that time Hietzing but now the 14th District, Penzing) at Hütteldorfer Straße 117.

A few years after Theodore was married, he was conscripted into the Austrian army and was sent to the Polish front. Here is a photo of my grandfather in his World War I Austrian army infantry uniform with my mother and grandmother.

Clara and Theodore were divorced on September 24, 1921. My grandfather, Theodore, was married two more times: in 1923 to Pauline Markstein (1884-1942: murdered at Riga) and then again in 1934 to Olga Stiassny.

I discovered wife number two only recently, with the help of Patrick Atlas, a descendant of the Atlas family, a family that was close to my grandmother. Pauline Markstein's first marriage, from 1907 to 1919, was to Juda Atlas. Theodore probably met Pauline while she was married to Juda and Clara's sister, Yetti, was married to Philip Atlas. My mother used to tell me that my grandfather was quite a character and had many girlfriends, which might have been the reason for the divorce from Clara and later from Pauline.

For 25 years, 1913-1938, Elsa and Clara lived together in the same apartment at Hütteldorfer Straße 117, located on the corner of Hütteldorfer Straße and Reinlgasse. My mother always told me that from her window on the third floor, she could look down Reinlgasse and see the Gloriette (a large, monumental, open building with columns and arches designed to glorify military conquests that was situated on the hill overlooking the Schönbrunn Palace) about 1 mile away from their apartment building.

Hütteldorfer Straße 117

Corner Reinlgasse and Hütteldorfer Straße
Source: Google Maps.

The Gloriette

Clara and Elsa in March 1932

After the divorce from Theodore in 1921, when Elsa was just 10 years-old, there were only the two of them living at the Hütteldorfer Straße apartment. It was clear from my grandmother's letters that mother and daughter had formed an incredibly tight bond.

My grandmother's last letter was dated November 17, 1941. The details of what happened to my grandmother through November 17, 1941, are described in her 1938-1941 letters, which make up Part I of this book. Whatever I know about the conditions under which she and my relatives lived during the period of the mass deportations from October 1941 to October 1942 comes from my research on conditions in Vienna during that time period. However, once the mass deportations began again in October 1941, Jewish life in Vienna was over. (See Appendix K for deportations.)

In August 1941, Clara was relocated to a collection-apartment building in the 2nd District, at Konradgasse 1. Until June 9, 1942, Clara continued to live at the Konradgasse 1 collection apartment. Although I don't have specifics about the last seven months of Clara's life, the situation for Viennese Jews became progressively worse during the period of the mass deportations, which probably had a profound effect on Clara.

Then on Tuesday, June 9, 1942, Clara was deported to Maly Trostinec on Transport 26. Based on historical information regarding the deportations to Maly Trostinec, my grandmother would have been ordered to leave her collection apartment at Konradgasse 1 and would have been loaded into a truck. Then she would have been transported to either a "collection site" at Kleine Sperlgasse 2 or directly to the Aspang train station, where she would have been crammed into a special train carrying 1006 persons in third-class passenger cars to Wolkowysk, Belarus; there the deportees would have been transferred to cattle cars.

The train designated Da 206 (Da stood for Star of David) traveled 1320 km (818 miles) and arrived at Maly Trostinec on Monday, June 15, 1942. The deportees were either dead on arrival or were murdered within one hour after arrival; if they had survived the train journey, they were herded into trucks and driven to the Blagovshchina Forest at Maly Trostinec, 12 km southeast of Minsk, Belarus. There they were shot, dumped into a ditch and covered with quicklime. The ditch was then covered with earth. About 10,000 Viennese Jews were murdered and buried at the Blagovshchina Forest at Maly Trostinec.

This was the sad and tragic end for my grandmother, Clara Bader Nichtern, whom I never even had the opportunity to meet and whom my mother couldn't talk about because of the emotional distress it caused her. But I was incredibly fortunate. I've gotten to know her well through her letters. She was a kind, gentle, welcoming and caring person who always wished the best for everyone around her – and all she wanted in life was to be reunited with her daughter, as she wrote, "…even if I could see you just one more time."

Leon (Leo), Amalia (Mali) and Markus (Maxl) Bader

Leon and Markus (Maxl) Bader sometime in the early/mid 1930s

Amalia, Mali, was the daughter of Fanny and Samuel Mihaly. She was born in 1898, in Vienna. She was married to Leon Bader, Clara's brother, in 1920. They had a son, Markus (identified in my grandmother's letters as Maxl), born in 1921.

Leon, Mali and Markus lived at Matzingerstraße 9 until their apartment was "Aryanized." When this happened, on October 6, 1938, they moved in with Clara at Hütteldorfer Straße 117. Mali left Vienna on March 22, 1939, and arrived in England on March 24, 1939. She took a job as a domestic for the Lux family, a job that my mother helped her obtain. After a few months with the Luxes, Mali went to work with Elsa at the vicarage in September 1939. On May 30, 1940, she was interned at Rushen Camp, Port Erin, Isle of Man and remained there for the entire war.

Early in March 1941, Leon and Markus Bader received a postcard from the Central Office that told them to report to the collection site at Kleine Sperlgasse 2, where they stayed for a week before they were deported.

On March 12, 1941, Leon and Markus Bader, along with 995 other deportees, were put on Transport No. 5 and deported from the Vienna Aspang Station to Opatow and Lagow, two neighboring small towns 50 km east of Kielce, Poland, which were part of the Radom District of the *General Gouvernement* in Nazi-occupied Poland.

Source: General Gouvernment – Wikipedia.

From my grandmother's letters, as of October 15, 1941, Leon and Markus were in Opatow. The ghettos of Opatow/Lagow, located in the Radom District of the *General Gouvernment*, were liquidated by the Nazis during the purges of October 20-22, 1942. Leon and Markus could have died from malnutrition or typhus during their stay at Opatow/Lagow or died during the liquidation of the ghettos, or they could have been sent to and killed at one of the death camps, such as Treblinka, that by 1942 surrounded the *General Gouvernment*.

Another possibility is that they could have been sent to the San-domierz labor camp, about 30 km southeast of Opatow, and died there. I have been trying to find out what happened to them, but as far as I know, there are no records of their deaths. In the records of the IKG, their death date is listed as May 8, 1945, which is the official end-date of World War II in Europe. That date was arbitrarily assigned when the actual death dates of victims could not be established.

Photograph of Mali Bader taken sometime in 1947

Mali Bader left the Isle of Man on May 25, 1945. I have no records of Mali's time in England after her release from the Isle of Man, but she returned to Vienna about 1947. On November 18, 1949, she married Bela Pordes. She died in Vienna in 1988.

Before the letters, what little I knew about my Aunt Mali came from some very brief conversations about how my mother got her aunt a job in England and left her mother behind in Vienna. She always thought that by helping her aunt get out of Vienna, she had missed the opportunity to get her mother out. Because of this, my mother suffered from massive guilt and would be overcome by emotion whenever she tried to talk about it.

But from the research that I have done, the odds of my grandmother getting out of Vienna were virtually zero: She was over 45, which disqualified her for a job as a domestic, eliminating that path (See Appendix H); she was identified as a Polish citizen; and as far as I know, she never obtained a *Heimatschein* – a certificate that Vienna, Austria, was her home – which would have designated her as an official citizen of Vienna: she applied for her U.S. visa in June 1939, which was too late. It was taking almost three years to obtain a visa, and the U.S. Consulate in Vienna closed in July 1941. I doubt that my mother knew or fully understood all of this.

I know my mother kept in touch with Mali because I found photographs of her and her second husband, Bela, taken at different times through 1975, and Mali's addresses over this time-period were in my mother's address books. But I don't recall ever meeting my Aunt Mali.

Rosalie, Benno and Max Spielmann, and Emma Spielmann Löff

Benno, Paul and Josefine Spielmann (ca. mid-1930s)

Rosalie Bader (1870-1944), the oldest of the Bader siblings, married Israel Spielmann (1871-1952) in Vienna in 1897. They had three children: Benno (1898-1945), Max (1902-1992) and Emma (1907-1943). Benno and Max were born in Vienna. Then they moved to Kirchberg am Wagram (about 60 km northwest of Vienna) sometime after Max's birth. Emma was born in Kirchberg am Wagram.

Benno Spielmann married Josefine (nickname Pepi) Heksch (1902-1944) in 1924. They had a son, Paul (1931-), whom my grandmother affectionately referred to as "sweet little Pauli."

Benno was an electrical technician. He and his wife also owned a grocery store and delicatessen. They were forced to relocate from the 16th District at Klausgasse 33 to the 1st District at Fleischmarkt 22, a few hundred meters down the street from the IKG offices. Benno worked at the IKG until the family was deported in October 1942.

Josefine's mother, Johanna Heksch (1870-1944) lost her apartment and moved in with them after they moved to Fleischmarkt 22.

On October 1, 1942, Benno, Josefine and Paul, along with Johanna Heksch, were deported to Theresienstadt; and on December 18, 1943, they were deported to Auschwitz. Josefine and Johanna were murdered in Auschwitz. Benno was sent to Buchenwald, where he was murdered in February 1945. Paul eventually ended up in Mauthausen. He was liberated in May 1945 and survived. After liberation Paul emigrated to Israel, where he changed his name to Shaul. Part II of this book is the story of how I found him.

Emma Spielmann married Adolf Löff (1902-1943) in 1926. They had a son, Kurt (1929-1943). More on them is given in the section on the Löff family, which follows.

Max stayed with his parents in Kirchberg am Wagram, where they lived until December 1938, when they were forced to relocate to an apartment in Vienna's 2nd District on Oberdonaustraße. In July 1939, they were again forced to relocate, this time to Konradgasse 1 in the 2nd District, a collection-apartment building, where they remained until their deportation in September 1942.

On September 24, 1942, Rosalie, Israel and Max were deported to Theresienstadt. Rosalie died in Theresienstadt, while Max and Israel, who had a chronic asthma condition, survived and emigrated to Sydney, Australia: Max in 1946 and Israel in 1947.

Max and Lilly Spielmann in Australia, date unknown.

Max Spielmann was married to Lilly Böhmer (1904-1998). I believe that they met each other while they were both living at the Konradgasse 1 collection-apartment building. They were deported to Theresienstadt on the same transport and were later married in Theresienstadt. After they were liberated, Max and Lilly emigrated to Sydney, Australia, and joined Lilly's brothers, who had been able to emigrate to Australia shortly after the *Anschluss*. Israel died in Sydney in 1952.

Max and Lilly had no children. Lilly had two nieces, who were very close to her, Evelyn (Evie) Koster Bowmer and Robyn (Robbie) Bowmer, one niece from each of her two brothers who had emigrated to Australia after the *Anschluss*. It was my contact with Evie and Robbie that eventually led me to Shaul.

Adolf, Emma and Kurt Löff

Adolf (Dolfi, 1902-1943) and Siegfried (1897-1943) Löff were the sons of Wilhelm Löff (1869-1934) and Louise Weiss (1870-1919).

Adolf (Dolfi) and Emma (Clara's niece) were married in 1926 and had a son, Kurt (1929-1943), referred to as Kurtl by my grandmother.

Before 1939, Dolfi, Emma and Kurtl lived in the 15th District at Wurzbachstraße 15. In July 1939, the family was forced to relocate to the

Photo of Adolf, Emma and Kurt Löff

9th District at Berggasse 19; interestingly, the house where they were placed was the former home of Sigmund Freud. In April 1942 they were relocated again, to a collection apartment at Novaragasse 4 in the 2nd District from where they were later deported.

Dolfi's brother, Siegfried, was married to Erna Fränkel (1901-1943). They had a daughter, Edith, who, on December 10, 1938, at age 13, was on the first *Kindertransport* from Vienna to London, along with 599 other children. Later, Erna and Siegfried also were relocated to Novaragasse 4.

Dolfi and Siegfried's cousin Egon Weiss moved to New York City in 1939 with his family and survived. In early 1941, Egon, with the aid of his nephew Herbert Löwenkron, who also had immigrated to New York City in 1939, and the support of a Mr. Asinoff living in New York City, was able to obtain affidavits for the Löff brothers and their families. Unfortunately, the affidavits got lost in the American consulate and were discovered about three months later.

However, by this time the "show-stopper" in obtaining a visa, provided your quota number was called, was the purchase of a ship ticket. This had to be paid for in advance in U.S. dollars. Because sending money to Vienna was very difficult and because the IKG had very little money and had substantially reduced its levels of financial support, a ship passage was very difficult to obtain: So, no money, no ticket! No exit from Vienna!

Adolf, Emma and Kurt, along with Siegfried and Erna, were deported to Theresienstadt on October 1, 1942. In January 1943 they were deported to Auschwitz, where they were murdered.

When Edith Löff arrived in England, she was placed in foster care. It was during that time that she met William Henry Harvey. They were married on October 14, 1945. They had a daughter, Ann, born on August 10, 1946. As of 1947, they were living at 71 Harold Road in South Chingford (now London). I have not been able to find any additional records for Edith and William. I found a death record for an Ann Harvey who died in 2005, but I am not sure it is for the daughter of Edith and William.

So far, I have not been able to locate any Löff relatives. I have spent the past three years trying to find a direct descendant of Siegfried or Adolf Löff so that I could tell them about the Stone of Remembrance for the Löff family that was dedicated in 2018.

Anna Spitz and her Brothers

Max (1864-1942), David (1875-1942), Anna (1882-1942), Nathan (1884-1940) and Jakob (1886-1907) were the five children of Marion Bader Sokal (Clara's aunt) and Berl Sokal. Max and David, who were born in Lemberg, and Anna, who was born in Vienna, were living in Vienna at the time of the *Anschluss*. David had four children, three sons and a daughter. His daughter died 18 years before the *Anschluss*. Max had no living children at the time of the *Anschluss*. The only information that I could find about Nathan came from my third cousin, Lydia Maier. I know nothing about Jacob.

In 1902, Anna married Adolf Spitz (1875-1934). They had three children: Carl (1903-1991), Grete (1904-1980) and Otto (1916-1984). All three left Vienna and survived. The two brothers left shortly after the *Anschluss*, Otto to Belgium and Carl to England. Otto married his wife, Cilli, in Belgium. Carl was married to Felicia in Vienna before their departure.

On February 4, 1940, Carl and Felicia left Liverpool, England, for the U.S. on the SS Nova Scotia. Carl and Felicia made their way to New York and then to San Francisco. Grete left Vienna in early 1939 and went to England to work as a domestic.

As was mentioned many times in my grandmother's letters, Anna Spitz suffered from severe depression and anxiety. Her condition worsened after Grete left Vienna. Anna also had heart issues and was confined to the cardiac ward of the Rothschild Hospital multiple times. I don't have any specifics about her death except that she died in the IKG hospital in Vienna on May 17, 1942, and was buried in *Zentralfriedhof* in Vienna.

Anna's two brothers, Max and David Sokal, were deported and murdered. On June 28, 1942, Max was deported from the old-age home at 10 Alxinger-gasse 97 to Theresienstadt on Transport 29. On June 14, 1942, David was deported to Sobibor on Transport 27. Two of David's three sons, Karl and Franz, survived the Holocaust. The third son, Fritz, a medical doctor, originally fled Vienna to France, but was arrested and confined in Drancy; and then on September 4, 1942, he was deported to Auschwitz and murdered.

All the children of Anna Spitz survived. Shortly after his arrival in New York City, Carl moved to San Francisco with his wife, Felicia, where they lived until their deaths, Carl in 1991 and Felicia in 1992. After the war, Otto and his wife, Cilli, returned to Vienna. They had two children, Anni and Peter. Both are married with children. Anni lives in Vienna, and Peter lives in Copenhagen. Grete returned to Vienna after World War II ended. She never married.

OTHER FAMILIES AND FRIENDS

In addition to the Bader and Nichtern families, there were two other families and four other persons who were very close to my grandmother and to my mother.

The Atlas Family

The Atlases were very close to the Baders in Vienna. Felix (Zelig) Atlas and his siblings were all born in Lemberg, Galicia. My guess is that the Atlas family and the Bader family knew each other when both families were living in Lemberg. Both the Bader and the Atlas families emigrated to Vienna. In the case of the Bader family, it was around 1883. In the case of the Atlas family, it was after 1891, as the youngest Atlas child was born in Lemberg.

Then in 1913 Yetti Bader married Philip Joachim Atlas. Unfortunately, Yetti died in 1918, without having any children. Philip remarried and had children. The Atlas family maintained a close relationship with Clara, probably because of the tie to Yetti and prior family ties. (Patrick Atlas, the grandson of Philip and his second wife, Antonia Gelbberger, tells me that we are related; but so far, I have not found the link.)

Philip's brother Juda married Pauline Markstein. They had two children, Richard and Gertrude, before they divorced. Gertrude (Trude) and Richard immigrated to the U.S. in 1939 and 1940, respectively. Trude was mentioned in my grandmother's letters as being very kind to my mother when Elsa arrived in America.

Other than that, I have no information on either of them except what I received from Patrick Atlas.

Pauline Markstein was the second wife of my grandfather, Theodore. My grandfather probably met Pauline during the time she was married to Juda, which overlapped the time that Yetti was married to Philip and the time that Theodore was married to Clara.

The letters regularly mention the relationship with Felix (1886-1967) and Ernestine (1889-1974) Atlas and their daughters: Gertrude (Trude, 1916-2003), Herta (1919-1996) and Edith (Ditta,1924-2014). All three daughters got married, Trude in England and Herta and Edith in New York. Later, Trude and her family immigrated to the U.S. They all had children and lived in the U.S. until their deaths.

My mother continued the relationship with Ernestine and Felix in New York City, especially during the first year after my mother's arrival. Felix established a furrier business, and, according to my grandmother's letters, my mother even purchased a fur stole from him. I suspect that the relationship gradually dissolved, although I don't know why, which may be the reason that Ernestine and Felix did not attend my mother's wedding. In any case, I have no recollection of the Atlas family, and I don't think I ever met them.

The Mihalys

Amalia (Mali) Bader (1898-1988) was the oldest of six Mihaly siblings. They were the children of Samuel (1873-1934) and Fanny Mihaly (1874-194?). The children were Amalia (Mali), Clara (1899-1921), Ernestine (Tinni, 1901-1964), Helena (Helli, 1904-?) Adolf (1906-2000), and Margarete (1910-1944, Auschwitz).

Margarete was married. Her married name was Beck. She had a daughter, Gertrude (Gerti or Trude,1928-1983) who was Margarete's daughter from her first relationship/marriage. From what I could tell from the letters, the Mihalys were very close to both my grandmother and my mother.

Margarete Beck was arrested by the *Gestapo* on September 21, 1943, because she was in a mixed marriage and was hiding her Jewish identity; and, as a Jew, she was violating the prohibitions on frequenting cinemas and taverns. Shortly after her arrest, Margarete was deported to Auschwitz, where she was murdered on January 13, 1944.

Grave marker of Gertrude Stergerits, daughter of Margarete Beck Source: BillionGraves.com

Gertrude went into hiding for two years as a "U-Boot" (literally, submarine), which was a term used to describe a person who went "underground" into hiding from the Nazis.

Eventually she was discovered, and in April 1944 she was arrested as a prostitute; she probably wasn't a prostitute, but the Nazis didn't have a category for "Jews in hiding." After her arrest, she was sent to Theresienstadt. She survived her internment. In searching for information about Gertrude, I found her grave at the New Jewish Cemetery in Vienna. I believe Gertrude was married to Leopold Stergerits. Gertrude's grave marker includes a memorial to her mother, Margarete Beck.

Besides Mali, Adolf, Ernestine and possibly Helena survived the Holocaust. I learned that Adolf had left Vienna. He married Julie Domingo (1920 -1996), born in Sidi Bel, Algeria. Before their deaths they lived in Antibes, in the French Alpes-Maritimes region.

The Fritz Saga

This was a huge surprise to me. I never knew that my mother had a serious, let alone a non-Jewish, boyfriend in Vienna. In any case, once Elsa left Vienna, the relationship slowly came apart. As far as I can tell, the Fritz saga ended in 1941.

I believe that Fritz's surname was Kaltenbrunner. (Unfortunately, when one hears the name Kaltenbrunner, one may think of the infamous Austrian and Nazi war criminal Ernst Kaltenbrunner, who was sentenced to death at the Nuremburg trials. However, I have not discovered a link between Fritz Kaltenbrunner and his family and Ernst Kaltenbrunner.) I was able to find an address in my mother's "little green book" with the name Kaltenbrunner and Fritz and an address, Goldschlagstraße 129, which was about 3½ city blocks from the Hütteldorfer Straße 117 apartment building where Elsa and Clara lived.

From my mother's "little green book"

When I looked up this address in the 1938 edition of the Lehmann's Vienna city directory, I found an Antonia Kaltenbrunner at that address. I believe that this was Fritz's mother.

Jakob Altenberg

Jakob Altenberg first appeared on the scene in August 1940, when Clara first met him during a visit to the hospitalized Uncle Bernhard. He played a vital role in my grandmother's survival in Vienna.

Jakob Altenberg owned a picture-frame-making factory and was an art dealer. He had historical significance as one of the three art dealers who sold the paintings of an unsuccessful young artist named Adolf Hitler during Hitler's time in Vienna, from 1907 to 1913. However, from the perspective of this story, he played an especially important role in the life of my grandmother.

Photo of Jakob Altenberg taken during the early 1900s
Source: Aganieszka Michalik

Although not a family member or a close friend of my grandmother, Jakob Altenberg was a very close and trusted friend of Julius Singer. Because of this relationship, Jakob became the person who provided my grandmother with a monthly stipend of 20-30 RMs for living expenses so that she could pay her rent and buy food. Julius's wife, Anna Nichtern Singer, was Elsa's aunt.

Originally, my grandmother had been getting monthly payments of 30 RMs per month from her former husband, Theodore. After Theodore left Vienna, the payments were provided by Theodore's sister and brother-in-law, Anna and Julius Singer. After the Singers left Vienna, the payments were then provided by Theodore's brother Bernhard. Sometime during the summer of 1940, Bernhard sustained an ultimately fatal head injury. During Bernhard's hospitalization, Jakob Altenberg showed up and told my grandmother, who happened to be visiting Bernhard in the hospital at that time, that he had been directed by Julius Singer to take over for Bernhard. I found out from my cousin Julie Metz, the granddaughter of Anna and Julius Singer, that Jakob and Julius had fought together in World War I, where they became the best of friends. Apparently, Jakob had access to some money so that he could provide my grandmother with her stipend, at least through November 17, 1941, the date of the last letter.

Through further research, I found out that Jakob died in Vienna on January 13, 1944, at the age of 69. He is buried in the *Zentralfriedhof* in Vienna.

Helene Diamand

Helene Diamand (1878-1942) was my grandmother's best friend and was regularly mentioned in the letters. Clara and her brother Leon, Helene Bergoffen Diamand and her brother Adolf, and Anna Sokal Spitz all grew up together in Vienna. Their close relationship was clearly evident in my grandmother's letters.

I don't have specifics about what happened to Helene Diamand, except that she was murdered in the Holocaust. I found a Page of Testimony that was submitted by her great niece, Hedy (Hedwig) Shneyer, in 1977. Hedy was the daughter of Oscar Bergoffen. Oscar was the son of Adolf Bergoffen, Helene's brother. Hedy came to the U.S. with her father and mother in 1939, when she was 17 years old. Hedy died in 1998. So far, I have not located a relative that I can contact.

Michel Salter

After Helene Diamand, Michel Salter (1880-1942?) was my grandmother's next-closest friend. He also was regularly mentioned in my grandmother's letters. He had a daughter, Elisabeth (Liesel), who left Vienna in 1939 to take a job as a domestic in England. She got married in England.

I have not been able to find any more information about him. There is a Michael Salter who was born in 1889. He was murdered in Sobibor in 1942. Possibly there could have been a transcription error and Michel and Michael could be the same person, but their birthdates are nine years apart. Michel's birth year was clearly given as 1880 in one of my grandmother's letters.

FROM THEN TO NOW: THE REST OF THE STORY

Preserving the memory of Clara Bader Nichtern

On May 18, 2014, I dedicated a Stone of Remembrance for my grandmother at the Konradgasse 1 collection apartment house. After my speech, a number of people came up to me. They wanted to let me know about a woman, Waltraud Barton, who founded the IM-MER (Initiative Malvine – Remembering Maly Trostinec) Association to commemorate the 10,000 Viennese Jews who were murdered at Maly Trostinec.

IM-MER organized meetings and gatherings to memorialize the Maly Trostinec deportation dates and, annually, has taken groups to the killing fields of Maly Trostinec, located about 12 km east of Minsk, Belarus.

I took down Waltraud Barton's contact information. Then, over the next few years, I was in regular contact with her and was able to work out a date when I could participate in a group trip to Maly Trostinec.

On May 24, 2017, I was at the Blagovshchina Forest killing fields at Maly Trostinec with Fran and our friend Carol Jackson. We were part of a group of 21 people, including a rabbi and a cantor, all brought together through the tireless efforts of Waltraud Barton. Not everyone there had a relative who had been murdered at Maly Trostinec; nor were they all Jewish. Some were there because they were Viennese and felt that they had a responsibility to help erase a terrible past by commemorating the Viennese Jews murdered and buried somewhere in the Blagovshchina Forest.

We conducted a funeral service for 61 Viennese Jews known to have been murdered at Maly Trostinec. I gave a eulogy for my grandmother. The other participants gave eulogies for their relatives or for those who no longer had living relatives or whose relatives could not make the trip.

Yellow Plaque for my grandmother on a tree in the Blagovshchina Forest at Maly Trostinec

We attached yellow plaques to the trees in the forest that grew on the grounds of the killing field. These yellow plaques symbolically represented the unknown graves that belonged to my grandmother and the 60 other victims we memorialized that day.

For me, the trip to Maly Trostinec was a way to get some closure for my grandmother and to give her the funeral service that she never had.

Dedication of Stone for Leon and Markus Bader

When we returned to Vienna after the trip to Maly Trostinec, we also dedicated a Stone of Remembrance for Leon and Markus Bader on Sunday, May 28, 2017, at the Hüttel-dorfer Straße 117 apartment building, their last known residence before they were deported to Opatow/Lagow. The Stone of Remembrance serves as the gravestone that they never had.

Stone of Remembrance for Leon and Markus Bader

October 17, 2015 - Fran and Irv meet Shaul's Israeli family

On the afternoon of Saturday, October 17, 2015, Fran and I arrived at Ben Gurion airport in Tel Aviv. This was my second trip to Israel. I had visited Israel once before, in December 2013, but at that time, I had no clue that I had family in Israel.

Since I had met Shaul in July 2014 at the home of his son, Benny, in Huntington Woods, Michigan, I wanted to spend part of this trip getting to know him and meeting a few of his family. We were met at the airport by Shaul and his son-in-law, Naor. Then Naor drove us to Maccabim, where Naor and Einat, Shaul's daughter, live. The plan, so we thought, was to have dinner there and after dinner go on to Ashkelon, where Shaul and his wife, Miriam, live.

Little did we know what was in store for us. After we were given a tour of Naor and Einat's beautiful contemporary home, we took the opportunity to relax for a while around their pool. As we were sitting there, drinking Naor's very good Israeli wine, family members continued to arrive – and arrive – and arrive. In fact, 26 members of the 36 members of Shaul's immediate and extended family arrived. We then spent an absolutely amazing evening with them.

Irv reviewing the family tree with Shaul's daughter Sigal and son Yuval

Dinner in Israel

I went over the research that I had done to find the Bader relatives and how they were related to the Spielmanns. All the family members were totally engrossed in trying to understand how the names of the people I showed them on a genealogy chart were related to Shaul. Like me when I started, they had no idea who these people were.

This went on for a few hours, after which we had an absolutely wonderful dinner, meeting with family members and drinking more excellent Israeli wine. There was enough delicious food for 100 people. It was a truly exceptional evening.

Then we spent Sunday with Shaul and his wife, Miriam, visiting their daughter Ayala and son-in-law Moshe at Kibbutz Yad Mordechai, named after the commander of the Warsaw Ghetto uprising. On Monday, we went to the town of Sde Boker, in the Negev desert, to visit Shaul and Miriam's son Yuval and daughter-in-law Liat. On Tuesday morning, Shaul took us for a tour of Ashkelon.

Meeting Evie and Robbie Bowmer

It was my contact with Evie and Robbie Bowmer, Lilly Spielmann's nieces in Australia, that eventually led me to Shaul. Fran and I met them in Sydney in March 2016. We spent a day with them and learned a lot about Max Spielmann and his relationship with Lilly.

Evie and Robbie gave me Max's wedding ring to give to Shaul, which I did when we next saw him the following year. The ring was constructed by Max in Theresienstadt, where he fashioned it from an iron nail. Max wore this ring until his death. I believe that Lilly had a similar ring.

Evie, Irv, Fran and Robbie in Sydney, Australia

Stone of Remembrance Dedication for the Löff family

On the morning of Thursday, May 3, 2018, Fran and I met my cousin Shaul, along with 10 of Shaul's immediate family. We gathered at the Löffs' last known address in Vienna, Novaragasse 4, in the 2nd District, to dedicate a Stone of Remembrance for Adolf, Emma and Kurt Löff, Shaul's aunt and uncle and their son, Shaul's cousin and closest childhood friend. We were joined by Carol Jackson,

Stone of Remembrance for Adolf, Emma and Kurt Löff

her cousin Janet Withers and Betsy Anthony, who, as a representative from the USHMM, was in Vienna for a conference. I took this opportunity to introduce Betsy to Shaul and his family, as the person without whom I probably would not have found him.

The Novaragasse 4 address was a deportation-collection apartment and was the Löffs' last residence before they were deported, on October 1, 1942, to Theresienstadt and ultimately to Auschwitz, where they were murdered. The Stone of Remembrance serves as the gravestone that Adolf, Emma and Kurt never had.

Stone of Remembrance Dedication for Benno and Josefine Spielmann

That afternoon the group of family and friends met again. We gathered at Börseplatz next to the Hermann-Gmeiner Park in the 1st District of Vienna. The Stone of Remembrance commemoration ceremony began about 3 p.m. and included speeches from local government officials and representatives from the Association of the Stones of Remembrance. After the initial ceremony at the park, we then proceeded to walk to the various Stone of Remembrance dedication sites for that day, all in the 1st District.

After two Stone of Remembrance dedication stops, we came to Fleischmarkt 22 to dedicate a Stone of Remembrance for Shaul's parents, Josefine and Benno Spielmann, at their last-known residence before they were deported to Theresienstadt on October 1, 1942. After Theresienstadt, the family was deported to Auschwitz, where Josefine was murdered in 1943. Benno was deported to Buchenwald and was murdered in 1945. Shaul was moved from camp to camp and survived a Death March before he was finally liberated at Mauthausen.

Standing in the interior courtyard of the building, surrounded by his family and friends from Israel, the U.S. and Vienna, Shaul spoke movingly about the horrors he and his parents had endured. He said that with his return to his last home in Vienna, his life had now come full circle, with the Stone of Remembrance serving as the gravestone that his parents, Benno and Josefine, never had.

Stone of Remembrance for Benno and Josefine Spielmann

Shaul Speaking in the courtyard of Fleischmarkt 22

The Now! – Shaul with Family and Friends

The next day, Shaul and the family that accompanied him to Vienna gathered together on the Ringstraße sidewalk in front of the Vienna Marriott hotel and across from the Stadtspark, with its famous statue of Johann Strauss. We took the family picture below.

Some of Shaul and Miriam Spielmann's children and grandchildren, as well as Irv and Fran Adler and friends Carol Jackson and Janet Withers, traveled to Vienna to attend the Stone of Remembrance dedications for the Löff and Spielmann families.

Pictured are:

Back row: Irv Adler, Shaul Spielmann, Rafi Berko, Naor El-Hay and Carol Jackson

Middle: Einat El-Hay, Fran Adler, Sigal Berko, Miriam Spielmann, Noam Spielmann, Noa El-Hay and Janet Withers

Front: Talia Spielmann, Roee El-Hay and Benny Spielmann (kneeling)

Shortly after our photo shoot, the Spielmann family group got into three SUVs and headed off to see the Mauthausen concentration camp, where Shaul had been a prisoner until his liberation on May 5, 1945.

Conclusion

With **THEN and NOW** we have tried to show the plight of the Jews of Vienna through the eyes of my grandmother and other relatives.

Regarding my family members, there were some specific stories and tragic themes that emerged:

- Discovering my grandmother and my lost Viennese family.
- The incredibly tight bond between my mother and her mother, my grandmother, and what a kind, caring and thoughtful person Clara was. It became clear to me why my mother was the same way.
- The Fritz story: the non-Jewish boyfriend whom my mother left behind in Vienna and who later became a Nazi.
- The tragedy of Mali and Maxl: a mother's desperate attempts to get her son out of Vienna and a son, equally desperate to get out, whose every attempt failed, eventually leading to deportation and death.
- Tante Spitz and the sadness, despair and sickness caused by knowing you will never see loved ones again.

Then there were the over-arching experiences and tragedies of the Vienna Jewish community as told through family members, friends and events:

- Hiding the truth about the events in Vienna.
- Desperation and inability to escape.
- Struggling to survive under oppressively worsening Nazi subjugation
- Determination to maintain hope and faith.
- Support from non-Jewish friends and acquaintances.
- Escape to England and then to the U.S.
- Role of the IKG in the lives of the Jewish community.
- Relocation of the Jews as a staging for deportation.
- Mass deportations starting in 1941 – implementation of the "Final Solution."

With all this terribleness as a backdrop, as we reach the 11th year of my saga, the hope and faith that ran though the letters persevered through the family members who survived, and can be seen daily in their children, grandchildren and great-grandchildren. And with **THEN *and* NOW,** I hope it will continue in subsequent generations of these families.

As for some final words, I can say that for me it has been an incredible journey. How would I ever have known that I had this large extended family living in Israel? And then to meet them!

When I took my first trip to Israel in 2013, I had no idea that the Spielmann family existed. When I met Shaul and his wife, son and daughter in July 2014, I was a bit overwhelmed to meet a family member who I hadn't known was alive a few months earlier, as well as his children. When I took my second trip to Israel in 2015, I discovered that I had many wonderful relatives living in Israel that I could visit. And since then, we have met again, both in the States and in Israel – and even in Vienna!

And during the past few years, we have memorialized the Bader relatives who perished in the Shoah. A few years earlier, I didn't know who they were. Now we have given them the memorial ceremonies and gravestones they never had.

As Shaul has reached his 90th birthday in July 2021, for me he is the living embodiment of what was **THEN and** what is **NOW**. I treasure the moments that I have had with him, and as Jews like to say, he should live to 120!

So, what more can I say, except that with everything that they went through, if they could see us today, my grandmother, Clara, and my mother, Elsa, would be overjoyed to see the descendants of the Baders living and thriving in Israel and that, after all these years, I found and reunited with "sweet little Pauli."

Acknowledgements

Since this book took more than ten years to write, there are a lot of people that I must thank. Their knowledge, research and support made this book a reality.

This journey began when Fran and I first walked into the office of Dr. **Elisabeth Klamper** at the DÖW. I must thank her for shocking my system and opening my eyes with respect to the fate of my grandmother and for her knowledge and support in helping me on the way. Over the years I have been regularly corresponding with Dr. Klamper. She has helped me clear up some of the mysteries that I discovered as I delved into the letters. We have met with Dr. Klamper many times, either at her office at the DÖW, or at a local restaurant or at a Viennese Kaffeehaus. She also has become a good friend to me and to my wife, Fran.

Then there is **Dr. Elizabeth "Betsy" Anthony**. Our meeting with her in June 2012 and her knowledge, guidance, friendship and empathetic support over these past years have been invaluable to me personally. Her research of the ITS (now Arsolsen) archives led me to finding my cousin, Shaul Spielmann. I regularly consulted with Betsy, a Holocaust historian, on the situation for Jews in Nazi Vienna and to get her insights on how to write this book. Fran and I have met with Betsy, in Washington, D.C., in Vienna and in Fort Wayne, when she came to give presentations on behalf of the USHMM. Even this past year, in the times of Covid-19, we have been able to talk with and see Betsy regularly with the help of Zoom technology. We were incredibly lucky to have met Betsy and then to get to know her.

I am indebted to the late **Dr. Elisabeth Ben David-Hindler, Daliah Hindler** and the **Association for the Stones of Remembrance,** founded by Dr. Ben David-Hindler, who passed away in 2016. The Association for the Stones of Remembrance gave me an opportunity to memorialize the family members who perished in the Holocaust. The Stones of Remembrance are the grave markers that these relatives never had. The dedication of a Stone of Remembrance for my grandmother also led to a chance encounter that eventually led to discovering the last surviving member of my Viennese family, my cousin Shaul.

I am indebted to **Waltraud Barton** and her work through the Association IM-MER. Her tireless efforts to remember the approximately 10,000 Viennese

Jews murdered at Maly Trostinec gave me a better understanding of the tragedy of Maly Trostinec and the opportunity to participate in a funeral service for my grandmother that provided some closure to her fate. Waltraud's extraordinary efforts over the past several years on behalf of the victims and their surviving families have been officially acknowledged by the Austrian government.

I must thank **Dr. Michaela Waggram-Blesch** and her colleagues for writing and publishing the book *Topographie der Shoah*, and **Professor Ilana Offenberger** of the University of Massachusetts-Dartmouth for writing and publishing the book *The Jews of Nazi Vienna*. These two scholarly works provided a great deal of historical information on the impact of the Nazi occupation and the persecution of the Jews of Vienna and put many of the events described in the letters into historical context, which helped me understand what happened to the Viennese Jewish population. In a similar vein, I must posthumously thank **Dr. Traude Bollauf** for her seminal work *Dienstmädchen Emigration*, about the women who fled Vienna in 1938-1939 to take positions as housemaids in England. This allowed me to understand how my mother, as well as other relatives, escaped Vienna and survived the Holocaust. If I had not discovered and read *Dienstmädchen Emigration*, I would not have understood how and why my mother was able to leave Vienna and the guilt she felt her entire life because she had to leave her mother behind.

Many thanks have to go to **Joy Gieschen**. It was Joy who identified the two different penmanship styles; who, while translating the *Lateinschrift* letters, discovered many of the names in the letters and how some of these names related to one another; whose job interview at the International School in Vienna led to the discovery of the Stones of Remembrance; and who, through her detailed analysis of the letters for her master's degree project, clearly showed the incredibly tight bond that existed between my mother and my grandmother.

And I offer more than many thanks to our good friend **Carol Jackson**. It became a labor of love for Carol to teach herself *Kurrentschrift*, to painstakingly transcribe all the letters that hadn't been transcribed and then to retranslate most of them. The result was a very good set of translated and analyzed letters that was used for Part I of this book. Carol developed such a strong bond with my grandmother through the letters that she went with us to Maly Trostinec and to the Stone of Remembrance dedication for Leon and Markus Bader in 2017, went with us to Benny Spielmann's home in Huntington Woods to meet Shaul later in 2017, and in 2018, met us in Vienna for the Stone of Remembrance dedication for Shaul's parents. Carol's insights into what my grandmother might have been thinking as she put her thoughts to paper have been invaluable.

I would like to thank **Marianne Salinger and Michael Simonson** of the Leo Baeck Institute in New York City for providing me with the initial translations of the letters written in *Kurrentschrift*. The translations of the *Kurrentschrift* letters provided us with a great deal of needed information from the period September 1938 to June 1940, starting from my mother's departure from Vienna.

I also would like to thank my cousin **Julie Metz**, the granddaughter of Julius and Anna Nichtern Singer, who put me in touch with the folks at Leo Baeck and who explained the relationship between Julius Singer and Jakob Altenberg to me; and to **Aganieszka Michalik**, Jakob Altenberg's great-great niece, who provided me with a photograph and details about his life; and my cousins, **Peter Spitz** and **Lydia Maier**, who gave me information on the Spitz and Sokal families.

I would like to thank **Dr. Patrick Atlas**, who provided me with detailed information on the Atlas family. Patrick's grandfather Phillip's first marriage was to my great aunt, Yetti, who died without having children. Then his grandfather remarried, leading to the birth of Patrick's father and then to Patrick. Patrick told me about my grandfather Theodore's second marriage to Pauline Markstein-Atlas, who had been previously married to Patrick's great uncle Juda. This was quite a revelation. My mother used to tell me that my grandfather, Theodore, was quite a character. My guess is that there was a lot more that she never told me.

"Ohne Fleiß Kein Preis! (No Pain No Gain!)" That is what **Dr. Suin Roberts** of Purdue Fort Wayne University said to me early on as she showed great patience and worked with me to improve my German reading and translating skills. Being able to translate German effectively became especially important as some of the research that I needed to do to understand the context of the letters required reading scholarly works on the Holocaust in Vienna, which were only available in German. Not only has Suin been a German instructor to me, she also has become a friend.

As I was doing internet research on the emigration situation in Vienna after the *Anschluss*, I came across a reference to a **Dr. Melissa Jane Taylor**, whose doctoral research was on the activities of the U.S. consulate in Nazi Vienna and how these activities were influenced by the U.S. immigration laws that existed at that time. From Dr. Taylor's analysis, it became clear that because my grandmother was considered a Polish citizen living in Vienna, her deportation was a fait accompli. It is my guess that my mother never fully comprehended this, and I probably would not have understood it either, had I not come across Dr. Taylor's research.

I must thank my volunteer editorial staff, consisting of **Dr. Talia Bugel, Dr. Steve Carr, Lisa Fybush, Betsy Gephart, Dr. Alexis Macklin, Donna Metrou, Dr. Suin Roberts and Beth Zweig** for taking the time to read and review the draft manuscript of this book. Each of them gave us a different view of what was written. All of them provided valuable critical insights, edits and suggestions that led to major changes in the structure and content of the book compared to its original draft. And an additional thank you goes to **Dr. Macklin**, whose support and assistance in making additional refinements helped us greatly on the road to getting this book published.

Thanks to **Blake Sebring**, whose explanations of his own experience helped me understand the publishing process.

I am indebted to **Amy Keller** for her talents, skill and creativity in converting our manuscript into a published book and for her good humor as we made many changes. Thanks also to **John Gevers**, for collaborating with Amy on the front cover of the book, which captures much of what this book is about.

I am also indebted to my longtime friend **Dr. Virginia Dilkes**, who has been encouraging me to write and publish this book from the time she heard about the letters and the family members I discovered.

Thank you to my son, **David Adler**, for his legal consultation, and thank you to him and my daughter, **Cara Adler**, for their continued support.

Last, but decidedly not by a long shot least, I have to thank my wonderful wife, best friend and companion, **Fran**, for her continued support as I struggled to write this book. Converting the writings of my grandmother and other relatives, contained in 102 letters, into the narrative, Part I of the book, was an extremely difficult task, as today what was in the letters could have easily been replaced by a series of telephone conversations between my grandmother and my mother. The letters were written as a stream of consciousness, sometimes over a few days, mentioning or discussing events that occurred the date of the letter or several days before or after, and many times with contributions from other immediate family members. Fran not only helped make the conversion to a narrative possible by her writing and editorial skills, but she also wrote many portions of the narrative. In short, I could not have written this book without her. And, as the grandchild of Holocaust victims and a child of survivors herself, she understands what this book is about.

Appendices

A. ANTI-JEWISH REGULATIONS
FROM MARCH 15, 1938, TO MAY 12, 1942

Source: Walk, J., Das Sonderrecht für die Juden in NS-Stadt, 2nd Edition. C.F. Müller, Munich, 2003.

1938

Mar.15:	Swearing of allegiance of public officials to the *Führer*. Jewish officials were not sworn in and were removed from their positions.
Mar. 31:	Professional prohibitions against Jewish lawyers and judges.
April 26:	Ordinance requiring Jews to register property valued over 5,000 RM.
April 29:	Exclusion of all Jewish students from Viennese secondary schools.
May 16:	Exclusion of all Jewish students from Viennese compulsory schools.
May 18:	Establishment of the Property Transactions Office in Vienna.
May 20:	Introduction of the "Nuremberg Race Laws"[36] into Austria.
June 24:	Police ordinance prohibiting Jews from entering park areas.
July 6:	Prohibition against wearing folk costumes.
Sept. 30:	Professional prohibition for all Jewish doctors.
Oct. 5:	The passports of all Jews were marked with a "J."
Nov. 11:	Prohibited from possessing weapons.
Nov. 12:	Ordinance for the recovery of the street scene – obligation for the remedy of the damages of the November pogrom [*Kristallnacht*].
Nov. 12:	Ordinance eliminating Jews from German economic life.

---

36   The Nuremberg Race Laws were antisemitic and racist laws that were enacted in Nazi Germany on September 15, 1935. The two laws were the Law for the Protection of German Blood and German Honor, which forbade marriages and extramarital intercourse between Jews and Germans and the employment of German females under 45 in Jewish households; and the Reich Citizenship Law, which declared that only those of German or related blood were eligible to be Reich citizens. Source: Nuremberg Laws - Wikipedia

Nov. 12: Prohibition against attending theaters, movies, concerts and exhibits.

Nov. 12: Enforcement of a reparation for *Kristallnacht*.[37]

Nov. 16: Prohibited from wearing uniforms.

Nov. 29: Prohibited from keeping carrier pigeons.

Dec. 3: Confiscation of the driver's license and vehicle registration.

Dec. 21: Exclusion from the profession of midwife.

1939

Jan. 1: Requirement to adopt additional names (Sara and Israel) and to carry a Jewish identity card.

Feb. 21: Requirement to hand over objects [made] from gold, platinum, silver, precious stones and pearls.

April 30: Limitation on the rental protection for Jews.

Sept. 1: Beginning of the war and curfew at 8 PM (Summer at 9 PM).

Sept. 20: Prohibition from possessing radio sets.

Oct. 24: Exclusion from the voluntary fire department.

Dec. 1: No special food offers on meat and butter as well as no cocoa and rice.

1940

Jan. 23: Revocation of the Reich clothing card (clothing and shoes).

Mar. 5: Prohibited from donating blood.

Mar.11: Labeling of the food ration cards for Jews. Prohibition on the purchase of non-rationed foods such as chicken and fish.

April 8: Expulsion from the *Wehrmacht* of "*Mischlinge* I. Grade" [2 Jewish Grandparents] and husbands of Jewesses and "*Mischlinge* I. Grade".[38]

---

37   The Nazi regime made an immediate pronouncement that "the Jews" themselves were to blame for *Kristallnacht* and ordered the Jewish community to pay reparations for the damage caused on *Kristallnacht*, which amounted to a 1 billion RM "atonement" levied on the Jews of the Reich. Source: Kristallnacht | Holocaust Encyclopedia (ushmm.org)

38   The term "*Mischling*" was used in Nazi Germany to denote persons with Jewish ancestry. Per the Nuremberg Race Laws, a "full Jew" was a person who had at least three Jewish grandparents. A person with two Jewish grandparents was also legally Jewish and was classified as a Jewish *Mischling* of the first degree. A person with only one Jewish grandparent was classified as a *Mischling* of the second degree. Source: Mischling - Wikipedia

April 10:   Barrier for release for Jewish KZ[39] prisoners for the duration of the war.

April 13:   Exclusion from private medical insurance.

April 24:   Guiding Principle for Jewish emigration:

- Jewish emigration in the areas of the Reich is to be intensified. However, Jews able to serve in the armed or work forces are forbidden to leave for European countries and especially for enemy countries.

- Extension of emigration to Palestine is unwelcome, for existing emigration strict conditions and supervision.

- No emigration of Polish (or former Polish) Jews who find themselves in concentration camps.

- No deportation of Jews to the *General Gouvernement* [occupied countries and territories]. Their voluntary emigration is forbidden.

May 4:   Jews are forbidden to leave their apartments in the period 1 April to 30 September from 9:00 PM to 5:00 AM, and in the period of 1 October to 31 March from 8:00 PM to 6:00 AM.

May 4:   Regulation based on the order by the *Reichspresident* about the declarations of Jewish property: Specifications about the notification of changes in property to be filed with the relevant office of revenue.

May 6:   Transportation of Jews to the *General Gouvernement*: Contrary to the regulation of 24 April 1940, the deportation of Jews to Poland is permitted, but the commander for the occupied zones in Poland must be informed in advance.

May 14:   Notification of changes in property based on the order about the withdrawal of Jewish assets: Due to par. 5 of the order dealing with the declaration of assets by Jews of 26 April 1938, Jews are obligated to register with the higher administrative offices every change in assets that reaches beyond the scope of a modest life or regular business dealings.

May 17:   Emigration of Jews – settlement of Jews for agricultural occupations: In order to increase the emigration of Jews, and for their professional preparation for it, Jews are allowed to be employed as helpers in agricultural enterprises and as gardeners.

---

39   "KZ" is an abbreviation for "*Konzentrationslager*, " which means concentration camp.

May 24:	Presentation of certificate of clearance from tax liability with requests for receipt of permission for foreign currency.
Sept. 10:	Cancellation of renter protection. [Rent control.]
Oct. 7:	Prohibition for the use of air raid shelters together with Aryan men and women.
Oct. 25:	Restriction of the admission of "*Mischlinge* I. Grade" to higher education.

1941

June 1:	All apartment changes in the interior of the city of Vienna must be approved by the Central Office for Jewish Emigration.
June 26:	Non-availability of soap provisions for Jews.
Aug. 7:	Further restrictions on the food allowance.
Aug. 7:	Prohibition for military fit men between the ages of 18-45 to emigrate.
Sept. 1:	Decree for the identification requirement with a Jewish Star by September 19, 1941.
Sept. 30:	Prohibition for "non-Aryan" Christians to be buried in Viennese Christian cemeteries.
Oct. 3:	Overall obligation for Jewish forced labor.
Oct. 23:	Prohibition for Jews to emigrate from the German Reich.
Oct. 24:	Prohibition of friendly contact between Aryans and Jews.
Oct. 31:	Legalized rules for Jewish forced labor.
Nov. 13:	Compulsory handing over of typewriters, calculating machines, copying machines, bicycles, cameras and binoculars.
Nov. 14:	Prohibition to purchase books.
Nov. 25:	Forfeiture of German citizenship for emigrated or deported Jews (XI. Ordinance of the Reich's Citizenship Law), whose property belongs to the German Reich.
Dec. 12:	Prohibition on the use of public telephones.

1942

Jan. 5:	Handover of fur and wool clothing as well as skis, ski and mountain boots.
Feb. 14:	Baked goods and cakes forbidden.
Feb. 15:	House pets forbidden.
Feb. 17:	Employment ban for newspapers and magazines – Jewish Bulletin excluded.
Mar. 3:	Marriages between "*Mischlings* Grade I" and "Aryans" are forbidden during the course of the war.
Mar. 13:	Identification requirement for a Jewish Star to be on the entrance door of a "Jewish" apartment.
Mar. 24:	Prohibition for the use of public transportation without police permission.
May 10:	Prohibition of extramarital relations from "*Mischlings* Grade I" to "Aryans."
May 12:	Aryan barbers/hairdressers are not allowed to serve Jews.

B. ELSA NICHTERN'S DOMESTIC PERMIT

On page 14 of my mother's *Reisepass* (passport) was her permit and police registration that allowed her to enter and stay in England. However, it was the stamp on page 15 of her *Reisepass* that allowed her to work as a domestic servant in England. It was dated August 22, 1939. My mother might have had another document or letter which guaranteed her position as a domestic servant prior to her exit from Vienna on September 12, 1938, but so far I have not found it.

Police Registration   *Domestic Permit*

C. THE LETTERS

No.	Date of Letter	From Whom to Whom
1	Sep 20 1938	Clara to Elsa
2	Sep 28 1938	Clara to Elsa
3	Oct 1 1938	Clara to Elsa
4	Oct 6 1938	Clara to Elsa
5	Oct 11 1938	Clara to Elsa
6	Oct 13 1938	Clara to Elsa
7	Oct 19 1938	Clara to Elsa
8	Oct 24 1938	Clara to Elsa
9	Oct 28 1938	Clara to Elsa
10	Nov 2 1938	Clara to Elsa
11	Nov 7 1938	Clara to Elsa
12	Nov 11 1938	Clara to Elsa
13	Nov 17 1938	Clara to Elsa
14	Nov 22 1938	Clara to Elsa
15	Nov 25 1938	Henni to Elsa
16	Nov 28 1938	Clara to Elsa
17	Dec 3 1938	Clara to Elsa
18	Dec 8 1938	Clara to Elsa
19	Dec 13 1938	Clara to Elsa
20	Dec 17 1938	Clara to Elsa
21	Dec 18 1938	Mali, Maxl and Clara to Elsa
22	Dec 27 1938	Clara to Elsa
23	Jan 3 1939	Clara to Elsa
24	Jan 9 1939	Clara to Elsa
25	Jan 13 1939	Clara to Elsa
26	Jan 18 1939	Clara to Elsa
27	Jan 25 1939	Clara to Elsa

No.	Date of Letter	From Whom to Whom
28	Jan 30 1939	Clara to Elsa
29	Feb 7 1939	Clara to Elsa
30	Feb 14 1939	Clara to Elsa
31	Feb 20 1939	Clara to Elsa
32	Feb 24 1939	Clara to Elsa
33	Mar 2 1939	Clara to Elsa
34	Mar 12 1939	Clara to Elsa
35	Mar 16 1939	Clara to Elsa
36	Mar 29 1939	Clara to Elsa
37	Apr 2 1939	Clara to Elsa
38	Apr 2 1939	Clara to Elsa
39	Apr 8 1939	Clara to Elsa
40	Apr 13 1939	Clara to Elsa
41	Apr 19 1939	Clara to Elsa
42	Apr 26 1939	Clara to Elsa
43	Apr 26-May 11 1939	Clara to Elsa
44	May 11 1939	Clara to Elsa
45	May 15 1939	Clara to Elsa
46	May 22 1939	Clara to Elsa
47	Jun 5 1939	Clara to Elsa
48	Jun 12 1939	Clara to Elsa
49	Jun 19 1939	Clara to Elsa
50	Jun 26 1939	Clara to Elsa
51	Jun 30 1939	Clara to Elsa
52	Jul 1 1939	Clara to Elsa
53	Jul 8 1939	Clara to Elsa
54	Jul 14 1939	Clara to Elsa
55	Jul 20 1939	Clara to Elsa
56	Jul 25 1939	Clara to Elsa

No.	Date of Letter	From Whom to Whom
57	Aug 2 1939	Maxl and Leo to Elsa
58	Aug 2 1939	Clara to Elsa
59	Aug 8 1939	Clara to Elsa
60	Aug 16 1939	Clara to Elsa
61	Aug 23 1939	Clara to Elsa
62	Aug 28 1939	Clara to Elsa
63	Dec 18 1939	Clara to Elsa
64	Dec 19 1939	Maxl to Mali
65	Feb 8 1940	Clara to Elsa
66	Apr 11 1940	Clara to Elsa
67	Apr 17 1940	Leo to Mali
68	Apr 17 1940	Clara to Mali
69	May 9 1940	Clara to Elsa
70	May 22 1940	Clara to Elsa
71	May 27 1940	Clara to Elsa
72	Jun 11 1940	Clara to Elsa
73	Jun 18 1940	Clara to Elsa
74	Jul 9 1940	Clara to Elsa
75	Jul 23 1940	Clara to Elsa
76	Aug 5 1940	Clara to Elsa
77	Aug 13 1940	Clara to Elsa
78	Early Sept 1940	Clara to Elsa
79	Sep 13 1940	Clara to Elsa
80	Sep 26 1940	Clara to Elsa
81	Oct 30 1940	Clara to Elsa
82	Dec 05 1940	Clara to Elsa
83	Jan 4 1941	Clara to Elsa
84	Feb 1941	Clara to Elsa
85	Mar 2 1941	Clara to Elsa

No.	Date of Letter	From Whom to Whom
86	Mar 11 1941	Mali to Maxl & Leo
87	Mar 16 1941	Emma Löff to Elsa
88	Mar 27 1941	Clara to Elsa
89	Apr 10 1941	Clara to Elsa
90	Apr 27 1941	Clara to Elsa
91	May 13 1941	Clara to Elsa
92	May 27 1941	Clara to Elsa
93	Jun 12 1941	Clara to Elsa
94	Jun 21 1941	Carl Spitz to Elsa
95	Jul 29 1941	Clara to Elsa
96	Aug 28 1941	Clara to Elsa
97	Sep 1 1941	Clara to Elsa
98	Sep 25 1941	Clara to Elsa
99	Oct 15 1941	Clara to Elsa
100	Nov 10 1941	Carl Spitz to Elsa
101	Nov 17 1941	Clara to Elsa
102	Nov 30 1941	Elsa to Clara

D. THE HÜTTELDORFER STRASSE 117 APARTMENT DWELLERS

Source: 1938 Lehman Directory, p. 789.

Residents of
Hütteldorfer Straße 117
Apartment Building

←Reinlgasse→

E. Fürst

H. Tomsicek

Café Breitensee

Freihofer A

Fürst R

Herreth A

Huber G

Karri J

Kepla F

Nichtern

Palla E

Pilz A

Prefina J

Schierer J

Seelenfried A

Starhcha E

Vörös J

E. NAMES IN THE LETTERS

(Not all are included in the narrative in Part I; if there are no remarks, I have no information about them other than their names.)

Names of people in the letters	Remarks
Joseph (Pepi) Adler	Elsa Nichtern Adler's husband and my father
Jakob Altenberg	Gave Clara money after Bernhard Nichtern was incapacitated; very close friend of Julius Singer
Frau Altenberg	Wife of Jakob Altenberg
Minna Ansche	
Frau Arm	Lived on Märzstraße, in Clara's neighborhood.
Mr. Asinoff	Supplied affidavits for Löff family
Ernestine Atlas	Very close friend of Clara and wife of Felix Atlas
Felix (Selig) Atlas	Husband of Ernestine Atlas
Herta Atlas	Daughter of Ernestine and Felix Atlas
Gertrude (Trude) Atlas	Daughter of Ernestine and Felix Atlas; took job as a domestic in England, later married in England
Edith (Titta) Atlas	Daughter of Ernestine and Felix Atlas
Yetti Bader Atlas	Sister of Clara Nichtern and first wife of Philip Atlas, brother of Felix Atlas
Moritz Atlas	Brother of Felix Atlas
Leon Bader	Brother of Clara Nichtern. He and his family lived with Clara after Elsa left
Amalia (Mali) Bader	Wife of Leon Bader, one of the Mihaly siblings
Markus (Maxl) Bader	Son of Leon and Amalia Bader
Frl. Bader	Assistant at a school where Elsa attended. (Not a relation to Elsa)
Trude Baeck	Friend of Clara
Frl. Wachta Bäkin	
Herr Bärenkopf	
Josefine Barisak	
Frau Barisek	

Names of people in the letters	Remarks
Frau Baron	Close friend of Atlas family
Frau Bauer	Worked at local drugstore
Margarete (Grete/Gretl) Beck	One of the Mihaly siblings
Gertrude (Trude) Beck/Baek	Daughter of Margarete Beck
Herr Behemsky	
Frau Bek	
Emma Bemer	
Adolf Bergoffen	Brother of Helene Diamand. He immigrated to America
Oscar Bergoffen	Son of Adolf Bergoffen. He immigrated to America
Berthold family	
Willi Blau	
Minar Blau	
Herr Chech/Czech	
Mrs. Cotter	Elsa's second employer in England, May 1939-February 1940; wife of the vicar
Frau Daum	
Frau David	
Helene Diamand/ Diamant	Clara's best friend
Herr Divorschak	
Frau Divorschak	
Mina Döll	
Hans Döll	Son of Mina Döll
Frau Dolleschal	
Frau Domischeck	
Herr Dorfwirt	Close friend of Theodore Nichtern

Names of people in the letters	Remarks
Frau Eckstein	
Frau Eisler	
Herr Engle	
Herr Epstein	Friend of Theodore Nichtern
Frau Epstein	
Frau Feuerwerk	Possible previous resident of Konradgasse 1 apartment that Clara moved to
Frau Fraenkel	
Hedi Freihofer	Resident of Hütteldorfer Straße 117
Frau Freihofer	Resident of Hütteldorfer Straße 117
Frau Freithammer	Midwife at birth of Maxl Bader
Rosi Frenzl	
Milli Freud	
Herr Fried	He received mail from his children in England through "back channels"
Frau Fried	
Herr Fuchs	
Frau Fuchs	Clara's former boss at a women's clothing factory at Rembrandtstraße 17
Frau Fürst	Resident of Hütteldorfer Straße 117
Herr Fürst	Resident of Hütteldorfer Straße 117
Walter Fürst	1941 NYC address: 550 West 144th Street, Apt 5
Herta Fürst	Sister of Walter Fürst
Julius Garfinkle	Helped the Nichterns get to the USA
Fanny Mann Garfinkle	Wife of Julius and cousin of the Nichterns
Mitzi Geier	
Frau Gerstl	
Frau Getsch	

Names of people in the letters	Remarks
Gilli	Companion of Herr Süss of *ESRA Verein* (Jewish social service agency)
Tante Gisa	Sister of Frau Johanna Heksch
Helen Goldberg	
Trude Goldberg	
Dora Goldberg	Daughter of Trude Goldberg
Lottie Goldberg	Aunt of Trude Goldberg
Frau Goldner	
Frau Greif	Aunt of Ernestine Atlas
Rachel Guji	
Fanny Gulisch	
Mitzi Gulisch	
Rosi Gulisch	
Reinhard Hammer	
Hanni Tant	Believed to be Fritz's aunt
Herr Hauser	
Johanna Heksch	Mother of Josefine (Pepi) Spielmann
Ignatz Heller	Uncle of Fanny Steiner
Herr Hericz	
Frau Hermann	Lived on Grassegasse, in Clara's neighborhood
Frau Herr	
A. Herreth	Resident of Hütteldorfer Straße 117
Herr Holser	
Herr Horberg	
Herr Huber	Resident of Hütteldorfer Straße 117
Frau Huber	Resident of Hütteldorfer Straße 117
Frau Hübner	
Frau Jam	Had Hütteldorfer Straße address

Names of people in the letters	Remarks
Frau Janach	
Herr Kaepka	
Antonia Kaltenbrunner	Fritz's mother
Fritz Kaltenbrunner	Boyfriend of Elsa before she left Vienna
Uncle Kaltenbrunner	
Minar Kappel	Married about November 1940 and moved to Ferdinandstraße.
Frau Kappel	
Frau Kari/Kary	Clara's former cleaning lady; lived at Missingdörferstraße, bought a dairy store.
Frau Karri	Resident of Hütteldorfer Straße 117
Frau Katzerl	
Frau Kaufmann	
Herr Keller	
Frau Kepla	Resident of Hütteldorfer Straße 117
Febus Kinberg	Friend of Theodore Nichtern
Frau Kinberg	
Kiraly family	Relatives of a friend of Anna & Julius Singer, a woman who had previously lived at Konradgasse 1 and had been deported
Herr Klausner	
Markus Kleiner	A person that Clara met at an old-age home
Herr Kleinfeld	
Frau Kohmer	
Frau Koltritch/Kotritsch	
Herr Koltritch/Kotritsch	
Herr Korn	Lived on Rembrandtstraße
Herr Kremser	
Frau Krifzky	A former boss of Clara

Names of people in the letters	Remarks
Frau Kuemmel	
Herr Kühnel	Shoemaker whose shop was on Hütteldorfer Straße
Frl. Kühte	Former classmate of Elsa
Frau Landau	
Herr Lau	Friend of Theodore Nichtern
Herr Leopoldi	
Emma Löff	Daughter of Israel and Rosalie Spielmann and wife of Adolf Löff; Elsa's cousin
Adolf (Dolfi) Löff	Husband of Emma Löff
Kurt (Kurtl) Löff	Son of Adolf and Emma Löff
Siegfried (Fritz) Löff	Brother of Adolf Löff
Erna Löff	Wife of Siegfried Löff
Edith (Ditta) Löff	Daughter of Siegfried and Erna Löff; was on first *Kindertransport* from Vienna
Herr Lohrberg	
Frau Lohrberg	Youngest sister of Frau Pinschowsky
Majerl/Maierl/Meierl Lohrberg	Friend of Leon, Mali and Maxl Bader and of Mihaly family
Herr Löwenkron	Cousin of Egon Weiss
Herr Lustig	Friend of Theodore Nichtern
Lux family	Mali's first employer in England
Frl. Wilhelmine Malter	
Frau Markowitsch	Lived on Beckmanngasse, in Clara's neighborhood
Pauline Markstein	Second wife of Theodore Nichtern
Gertrude (Trude) Markstein	Daughter of Pauline Markstein from her first marriage
Richard Markstein	Son of Pauline Markstein from her first marriage
Fanny Mihaly	Mother of the Mihaly siblings
Adolf (Dolfi) Mihaly	Son of Fanny Mihaly

Names of people in the letters	Remarks
Gertrude (Trude/Gerti) Mihaly	Daughter of Margarete Mihaly Beck from her first marriage; kept Mihaly name
Ernestine (Tinni) Mihaly	One of the Mihaly siblings
Frau Milk	
Herr Milk	
Frieda Mok/Mock	
Walter Mok	Son of Frieda Mok
Toni Musil	
Herr Neff	
Herr Nemet	
Frau Nemetz	
Clara Bader Nichtern	My grandmother, Elsa's mother and Theodore Nichtern's first wife
Elsa Nichtern [Adler]	My mother, the daughter of Theodore and Clara Nichtern
Theodore Nichtern	My grandfather, Elsa's father, husband of Clara and one of the Nichtern siblings
(Joseph) Bernhard Nichtern	One of the Nichtern siblings and Elsa's uncle
Olga Nichtern	Theodore's third wife and mother of Henny Spitzer
Edith Nichtern	Daughter of Julius and Emile Nichtern; shortly after Anschluss, traveled to England with Fritz and Dolfi Singer
Julius Nichtern	One of the Nichtern siblings and Elsa's uncle
Emile (Millie) Nichtern	Wife of Julius Nichtern; took job as a domestic in England
Salamon (Rolf) Nichtern	One of the Nichtern siblings and Elsa's uncle
Karl Nuechtern	One of the Nichtern siblings and Elsa's uncle
Emma Oswald	
Wki (Vicki) Oswald	

Names of people in the letters	Remarks
Herr Palla	Resident of Hütteldorfer Straße 117
Frau Palla	Resident of Hütteldorfer Straße 117
Peter Palla	Child of the Pallas
Frau Patak	
Herr Patak	Friend of Theodore Nichtern
Otto Patscha	
Frau Patscha	
Tante Pauli	
Dr. Pik	
A. Pilz	Resident of Hütteldorfer Straße 117
Frau Pinschowsky	
Oskar Pinschowsky	
Rosa Poldi	
Franz Poldi	
Frau Pollmeier	
J. Prefina	Resident of Hütteldorfer Straße 117
Frau Pressing	
Gerti Prohaska	
Mitzi Prohaska	Close friend of Elsa
Schenni Prohaska	Close friend of Elsa
Herr Protowinsky	Local dentist
Frau Protowinsky	
Frau Pulitzer	
Frau Raschek	
Franzi Reauck	Person to whom Clara sold her furniture because of forced relocation to Konradgasse 1
Herr Reich	Friend of Theodore Nichtern
Willi Reichsfeld	

Names of people in the letters	Remarks
Frau Reichsfeld	
Reinharz	
Herr Reitl/Reitel	Owner of hat-making shop in Breitensee neighborhood frequented by Theodore Nichtern
Franzi Rosi	
Ernst Roth	
Frau Roth	
Martha Roth	Emigrated to Shanghai
Herr Rudolf	
Frau Sahan	
Michel Salter	Close friend of Clara since childhood; also had a son, but no name given.
Elisabeth (Liesel) Salter	Daughter of Michel Salter; took a job as a domestic in England, later married in England
Herr Schandl	Died on April 14, 1941 at age 71
Frau Schandl	
Anschi Schandl	Daughter of Herr & Frau Schandl
Edith Schenkelbach	
Frl. Emmi Scheuer	Had Grosse Mohrengasse address
Frau Schierer	Resident of Hütteldorfer Straße 117
Herr Schierer	Resident of Hütteldorfer Straße 117
Frau Schliesse	
Max Schlossfeld	
Frau Schmerek/Schmerck	Knew Elsa as a child
Frau Schmied	
Frau Schneider	Former teacher of Elsa
Herr Schorr	Was able to escape from Vienna; believed to have attended Elsa's wedding
Herr Schubert	Owner of photo studio on Breitenseerstraße

Names of people in the letters	Remarks
Herr Schwagner	
Frl. Schwartz	Representative of IKG welfare department.
Putzi Schwinkeles	
A. Seelenfried	Resident of Hütteldorfer Straße 117
Grete Segal	
Helene Segal	
Siegerl family	Close friends of Anna and Julius Singer
Anna Singer	One of Nichtern siblings and mother of Adolf, Siegfried and Eva Singer; provided money to Clara
Julius Singer	Husband of Anna Singer
Siegfried (Fritz) Singer	Oldest child of Anna and Julius Singer; shortly after Anschluss, traveled to England with brother and Edith Nichtern
Adolf (Dolfi) Singer	Second oldest child of Anna and Julius Singer; shortly after Anschluss, traveled to England with brother and Edith Nichtern
Hugo Singer	Unrelated person who knew Leon and Mali Bader
David Sokal	Brother of Anna Spitz and first cousin of Clara
Max Sokal	Brother of Anna Spitz and first cousin of Clara
Erwin Spendel/Spendal	Friend of Maxl Bader
Herr Spendel/Spendal	
Frau Spendel/Spendal	
Rosalie (Sali) Spielmann	Sister of Clara, mother of Benno and Max Spielmann and Emma Löff
Israel Spielmann	Husband of Rosalie, father of Benno and Max Spielmann and Emma Löff
Benno Spielmann	Oldest son of Israel and Rosalie Spielmann and Elsa's cousin
Josefine (Pepi) Spielmann)	Wife of Benno Spielmann

Names of people in the letters	Remarks
Paul (Pauli) Spielmann	Son of Benno and Josefine Spielmann
Max Spielmann	Youngest son of Israel and Rosalie Spielmann and Elsa's cousin
Anna Spitz	First cousin of Clara and mother of Carl, Otto and Grete Spitz
Carl Spitz	Oldest son of Anna Spitz; emigrated to San Francisco
Felicia (Fella) Spitz	Wife of Carl Spitz
Grete Spitz	Daughter of Anna Spitz; took a job as a domestic in England
Otto Spitz	Youngest son of Anna Spitz; shortly after Anschluss, emigrated to Belgium, where he remained during WWII
Caecille (Cilli) Spitz	Wife of Otto Spitz
Henrietta (Henni/Henny) Spitzer	Elsa's stepsister, daughter of Olga Nichtern from her second marriage; took job as a domestic in England
Frau Springler	
Frau Sprinzeles	
Herr Sprinzeles	
Grete Stadler	A person whom Clara and Elsa knew and Elsa saw in NYC
Frau Stadler	
Anschi Starhcha	Resident of Hütteldorfer Straße 117
Heide Starhcha	Resident of Hütteldorfer Straße 117
Joseph Steiner	
Hanni Steiner	
Max Steiner	
Frl. Fanny Steiner	Clara's roommate after relocation to Konradgasse 1
Frau Stern	

Names of people in the letters	Remarks
Sulzer	
Herr Süss	Worked at *ESRA Verein* (Jewish social services agency)
Herr Töpfner	
Frau Töpfner	
Mrs. Turle	Elsa's first employer in England, September 1938-May 1939
Herr Vogelkrammer	
Frau Vogelkrammer	
Herr Vörös	Resident of Hütteldorfer Straße 117
Alfi Vörös	Conscripted into army
Max Vortrefflich	Acquaintance of Clara
Eigner Wachmann	Friend of Theodore Nichtern
Tante Wachtel	Childhood friend of Rosalie Spielmann and eldest sister of Lottie Goldberg
Frau Weinmann	At one time worked with Clara in a tailor shop
Dr. Weisberg	A person whom Clara knew when he lived in Vienna and who emigrated to NYC
Egon Weiss	Adolf Löff's first cousin; left Vienna with his family in July 1939
Anschi Wicha	
Herr Wikugal	Friend of Theodore Nichtern
Frau Wilk	
Herr Wilk	
Herr Willig	
Frau Erna Willig	
Frau Wissel	
Herta Witschak	
Fritz Witschak	

Names of people in the letters	Remarks
Frau Wittmann	
Frau Wohlmut	Believed to be Hanni Tant, Fritz's aunt
Herr Wohlmut	Believed to be Hanni Tant's husband
Siegfried Wollner	
Frau Zinka	

F. IMPORTANT DATES IN THE REICH

Source: Dates extracted from references given in Appendix L.

1938

Mar. 13:	The *Anschluss*.
Mar. 18:	The IKG is closed after a *Gestapo* raid.
Mar. 26:	Göring gives a speech at the Northwest Railroad Station on the elimination of Jews from the economy in 4 years.
Apr. 1:	The transport of prominent Jews from Vienna to Dachau.
May 20:	Eichmann reopens the IKG and the *Zionistische Rundschau* is published.
May 20:	The Nuremberg Race Laws are introduced.
May 23:	Clara submits her Emigration Questionnaire.
May 25-27:	2,000 Jews are arrested in Vienna and sent to Dachau.
June 3:	The IKG opens the Emigration Department.
June 3:	The *Zionistische Rundschau*[40] publishes an article about emigrating to England as a household domestic.
June 4:	Sigmund Freud leaves Vienna.
June 14:	The Vienna city administration orders the elimination of Jewish renters from community buildings.
June 24:	Police issue an ordinance prohibiting Jews from entering parks.
July 6:	The Evian Conference is held.[41]
Aug. 20:	The Central Office for Jewish Emigration is established.
Sept. 12:	Elsa leaves Vienna.
Sept. 16:	Elsa arrives in England and registers with the police.
Sept. 29:	Britain, France, Italy and Germany sign the Munich Agreement.

---

40   See footnote 9 on page 14.
41   Delegates from 32 countries and representatives from refugee aid organizations attended the Evian Conference in Evian, France. They discussed options for settling Jewish refugees fleeing Nazi Germany as immigrants elsewhere in Europe, the Americas, Asia, and Australia. The United States and most other countries, however, were unwilling to ease their immigration restrictions.
Source: USHMM.org

Sept. 30:	Jewish doctors are excluded from the medical profession.
Oct. 1:	The Nazis march into the Sudetenland.[42]
Oct. 5:	All passports belonging to Jews are stamped with a red "J."
Oct. 28:	17,000 Polish Jews are expelled from the Reich.[43]
Nov. 9:	The *Zionistische Rundschau* ceases publication.
Nov. 9:	*Kristallnacht* (often referred to as the November Pogrom).
Nov. 12:	Jews are prohibited from going to theaters, movies, concerts and exhibits.
Nov. 12:	Ordinance for the elimination of Jews from economic life is issued.
Nov. 13:	Göring announces that the Jewish community must pay 1 Billion RM for *Kristallnacht* damages.
Dec. 10:	The first *Kindertransport* leaves Vienna.
Dec. 28:	Göring abolishes rent control for Jews.

1939

Mar. 1:	The relocation to Jewish homes and collection apartments begins.
Sept. 1:	The German Army invades Poland.
Sept. 3:	Britain and France declare war on Nazi Germany. (The "phony war" runs from September 1939 to May 1940.)
Sept. 3:	Britain declares German and Austrian refugees as "enemy aliens."
Oct. 17:	The first transport of Jews leaves Vienna for Nisko, Poland.
Nov. 1:	Germany annexes Poland into the German Reich.
Dec. 27:	Elsa's transit visa is extended to June 27, 1940.

---

42   The Sudetenland is the historical German name for the northern, southern, and western areas of former Czechoslovakia which were inhabited primarily by Sudeten Germans. These German speakers had predominated in the border districts of Bohemia, Moravia, and Czech Silesia since the Middle Ages. Source: Sudetenland - Wikipedia
43   From Oct 27-29, the NS-Authorities in Germany arrested approximately 17,000 Polish Jews and cancelled their German permits of residence After being arrested, they were stripped of any personal property or money and put on trains. These trains brought the deportees to the Germany–Poland border. Most of the 17,000 expelled Jews would remain in refugee camps on the border for almost a year. Source: Polenaktion - Wikipedia

1940

Feb. 16:	Elsa leaves England for the U.S.
Mar. 3:	Elsa arrives in Boston and goes on to New York City.
May 8:	Jews are forbidden to access public parks.
May 10:	Nazi Germany invades Belgium and France.
May-June:	Britain arrests German and Austrian refugees living in Britain as "enemy aliens." Many are interned on the Isle of Man and other locations. During 1941 many are released, but some remain, mainly on the Isle of Man.
June 10:	Italy enters World War II.
June 22:	France is divided.
July 10-Oct 31:	The Battle of Britain
Aug. 1:	The NS-Authorities establish the VUGESTA, the *Gestapo* Office for the Disposal of the Property of Jewish Emigrants.
Sept. 1:	The last legal transport leaves for Palestine.
Sept. 7:	The start of the "Blitz," the intense bombing of London by the *Luftwaffe*. It continues through May 1941.
Nov. 1:	Registration of Jews for the continuation of the food ration card.
Dec. 3:	Hitler approves the deportation of Jews from Vienna to the *General Gouvernement* in Poland.

1941

Jan. 8:	The Reich's Main Security Office in Berlin decides to deport 10,000 Jews from Vienna to the *General Gouvernement*.
Feb. 7:	The IKG emigration training courses end.
Feb.-Mar.:	First 5 mass deportations from Vienna.
May 15:	The Palestine Office closes.
May 21:	The order to concentrate all Jews to the 2nd, 9th and 20th Districts is issued.

June 1:	The resettlement of all Jews into collection apartments begins.
June 22:	Nazi Germany invades the Soviet Union.
July 9:	The U.S. Consulate in Vienna closes.
Aug. 27:	Clara is forced to relocate from Hütteldorfer Straße 117 to Konradgasse 1.
Sept. 1:	Jews are prohibited from leaving their residence without a permit.
Sept. 19:	Jews over 6 years old are required to wear the yellow star.
Oct. 3:	All youths 14 years or older who are not working for the IKG are required to do forced labor.
Oct. 15:	Mass deportation to the east restarts.
Oct. 23:	All Jewish emigration from the Germain Reich is completely forbidden.

G. DOCUMENTS REQUIRED TO LEAVE GERMANY

Source: www.USHMM.org

After 1937, Jews needed the following documents from German authorities to leave the country.

- Passport
- Certificate from the local police noting the formal dissolution of residence in Germany
- Certificate from the Reich Ministry of Finance approving emigration, which required:
  - Payment of an emigration tax of 25 percent on total assets valued at more than 50,000 RM. This tax came due upon the dissolution of German residence.
  - Submission of an itemized list of all gifts made to third parties since January 1, 1931. If their value exceeded 10,000 RM, they were included in the calculation of the emigration tax.
  - Payment of a capital transfer tax of 25 percent (levied only on Jews) of assets in addition to the emigration tax.
  - Certification from the local tax office that there were no outstanding taxes due.
  - Certification from a currency exchange office that all currency regulations had been followed. An emigrant was permitted to take 2,000 RM or less in currency out of the country. Any remaining assets would be transferred into blocked bank accounts with restricted access.
- Customs declaration, dated no earlier than three days before departure, permitting the export of itemized personal and household goods. This declaration required:
  - Submission of a list, in triplicate, of all personal and household goods accompanying the emigrant stating their value. The list had to note items acquired before January 1, 1933, those acquired since January 1, 1933, and those acquired to facilitate emigration.
  - Documents attesting to the value of personal and household goods, and written explanations for the necessity of taking them out of the country.
  - Certification from a currency exchange office permitting the export of itemized personal and household goods, dated no earlier than 14 days before departure.

- With the preceding documents, emigrants could leave Germany, if and only if they had valid travel arrangements and entrance visas for another country.

After the union of Germany and Austria in March 1938, emigrants from Austria holding an Austrian passport had to apply for a German exit visa before they were permitted to leave the country.

H. REQUIREMENTS FOR DOMESTIC WORK IN ENGLAND

Source: "Bulletin of the Co-ordinating Committee for Refugees," February 1939, p. 15.

A permit to be admitted to take up domestic work is granted on the following conditions:

(a) The applicant must have a medical certificate showing that she is healthy and capable for work.

(b) She must be a single, widowed or divorced woman between the ages of 18 and 45.

(c) Married women are accepted only if the husband is already in the United Kingdom.

(d) Married couples between the ages of 18 and 45 are accepted provided that both are to be employed on domestic work in the same household.

(e) The work undertaken by the applicant must be in a private household. She is not permitted to accept a post in any institution working for profit.

(f) Single men are not permitted to undertake private domestic work. An exception is sometimes made to this rule in the case of a highly skilled man wishing to undertake very specialized work, e.g., a highly qualified chef or pastrycook.

(g) "Au pair" arrangements are definitely not allowed.

(h) The minimum wage paid to a woman domestic worker must be 15s. a week in addition to board, lodging and laundry; and to a married couple must be £100 per annum in addition to board, lodging and laundry.

I. U.S. IMMIGRATION POLICY
DURING THE TIMEFRAME OF THE LETTERS

Source: https://encyclopedia.ushmm.org/content/en/article/united-states-immigration-and-refugee-law-1921-1980

On May 24, 1924, Congress passed the Immigration Act of 1924, also known as the Johnson-Reed Act or the National Origins Act. The act was meant to solve the "midnight races" problem and establish a more permanent immigration law. It created new quotas, which heavily favored England and northern Europe and set much lower quotas for immigrants from southern and eastern Europe, who had made up the majority of more recent immigration. The new law reflected anti-Catholic and anti-Semitic sentiment in the country. The 1924 law capped quota immigration at 164,667 people per year. Immigrants from the Western Hemisphere, needed for U.S. labor, were "non-quota" arrivals, exempted from the quota system.

The Johnson-Reed Act also mandated that potential immigrants present their paperwork and receive U.S. immigration visas at consulates abroad, prior to leaving for the United States. The State Department, therefore, became responsible for enforcing the quota law, and "midnight races" ended. In 1929, immigration was further limited to a total of 153,879 and the new quotas were re-calculated using complicated math based on the existing "national origins" of the population as reflected in the 1920 census and the new immigration cap. As a result, the quota for the British Isles rose from 34,007 to 65,721, while the quota for Germany fell significantly, from 51,227 to 25,957. Other countries fared worse: Poland, with a prewar Jewish population of 3.5 million, had a quota of 6,524, and Romania, with a Jewish population of nearly a million, had a quota of 377.

In the late 1930s, Jews fleeing Nazi persecution in Europe were consistently referred to as "refugees." However, this term had no legal meaning under U.S. law, save for theoretically exempting these immigrants from having to pass a literacy test.

Throughout the 1930s, most Americans opposed changing or adjusting the Johnson-Reed Act, fearing that immigrants, including those fleeing persecution, would compete for scarce jobs and burden public services in the midst of the Great Depression. (Later on, they would see them as a potential national security risk.) Consistent with overall anti-immigrant sentiments in the country, the State Department viewed the quotas as limits, rather than goals, and did not seek to fill the quotas. Between 1933 and 1941, for example, roughly 118,000 German quota slots that could have been used went unfilled.

After Germany's annexation of Austria and with the advice of the State Department, a group of Jewish congressmen met and decided not to introduce any new legislation to expand immigration to aid Jewish refugees. Public anti-immigration sentiment remained strong — in May 1938, only 23% of Americans were in favor of the immigration of German refugees — and these congressmen believed that legislation reducing immigration would prevail if the subject came up for debate. Several bills were introduced to aid refugees; many more were introduced to curb or end immigration. None passed. The only significant attempt to pass a law to aid refugees came in 1939, when Democratic Senator Robert Wagner of New York and Republican Congresswoman Edith Rogers of Massachusetts introduced legislation in both houses of Congress that would allow 20,000 German refugee children under the age of 14 into the country over two years outside of the immigration quotas. The legislation never made it out of committee for a vote.

After World War II began in 1939, the State Department cautioned consular officials to exercise particular care in screening applicants: "In view of the international situation, it is essential that all aliens seeking admission into the United States, including both immigrants and nonimmigrants, be examined with the greatest care." Visa applicants were required to submit moral affidavits, attesting to their identities and good conduct, from several responsible disinterested persons, in addition to financial affidavits.

Fears of infiltration and espionage led to additional restrictions on visa applicants. On June 5, 1941, diplomats abroad were cautioned that visas would soon be denied to applicants with close relatives remaining in German-occupied countries. American officials were concerned that unfriendly governments would use family members as hostages or bargaining chips to coerce immigrants to commit acts of sabotage or espionage.

On July 1, 1941, the same day that the new "relatives rule" went into effect, the State Department centralized all alien visa control in Washington. Visa applications were placed before an interdepartmental review committee consisting of representatives of the Visa Division, Immigration and Naturalization Service, FBI, Military Intelligence Division of the War Department, and the Navy Department's Office of Naval Intelligence. At this time, documentary requirements were also increased: applicants now needed two financial affidavits instead of one. U.S. consulates in Nazi-occupied territory shut down in July 1941. (This happened just as the systematic, mass murder of the Jews began with the German invasion of the Soviet Union.) For most Jewish refugees, the new paperwork combined with the lack of access to American diplomats ended their hope of immigration to the United States.

J. DOCUMENTS REQUIRED TO ENTER THE U.S. FROM GERMANY

Source: www.USHMM.org

In the years immediately preceding U.S. entry into World War II, potential immigrants were required to file the following documents to obtain a U.S. visa.

- Visa application (Form BC)—Five copies
- Birth certificate—Two copies (country of birth determined applicable quotas)
- Quota number, which established the person's place on the waiting list to enter the United States
- Two sponsors (close relatives of prospective immigrant were preferred). The sponsors had to be American citizens or have permanent resident status, and they had to fill out and provide the following:
  - Affidavit of Support and Sponsorship (Form C)—Six copies, notarized
  - Certified copy of most recent federal tax return
  - Affidavit from a bank about accounts
  - Affidavit from any other responsible person regarding other assets (affidavit from the sponsor's employer or statement of commercial rating)
- Certificate of Good Conduct from German police authorities, including two copies of each of the following:
  - Police dossier prison record
  - Military record
  - Other government records about the individual
  - Affidavits of Good Conduct (after September 1940)
- Evidence of passing a physical examination at a U.S. consulate
- Proof of permission to leave Germany (imposed September 30, 1939)
- Proof the prospective immigrant had booked passage to the Western hemisphere (imposed September 1939)

K. DEPORTATIONS FROM ASPANG RAILROAD STATION

Gesamtverzeichnis der Deportationstransporte vom Wiener Aspangbahnhof [1]

Complete list of deportation transports from Aspang Railway Station, Vienna [2]

DATUM / DEPORTATIONSZIEL / ZAHL DER DEPORTIERTEN DATE / DEPORTATION DESTINATION / NUMBER OF DEPORTEES			DATUM / DEPORTATIONSZIEL / ZAHL DER DEPORTIERTEN DATE / DEPORTATION DESTINATION / NUMBER OF DEPORTEES		
20. Oktober 1939	Nisko am San	912	05. Juni 1942	Izbica	1001
26. Oktober 1939	Nisko am San	672	09. Juni 1942	Maly Trostinez	1006
15. Februar 1941	Opole	996	14. Juni 1942	Sobibor	996
19. Februar 1941	Kielce	1010	20. Juni 1942	Theresienstadt	996
26. Februar 1941	Opole	1049	28. Juni 1942	Theresienstadt	983
05. März 1941	Modliborzyce	981	10. Juli 1942	Theresienstadt	993
12. März 1941	Lagow/Opatow	995	14. Juli 1942	Theresienstadt	988
15. Oktober 1941	Litzmannstadt	1005	17. Juli 1942	Auschwitz	995
19. Oktober 1941	Litzmannstadt	1003	22. Juli 1942	Theresienstadt	1005
23. Oktober 1941	Litzmannstadt	991	28. Juli 1942	Theresienstadt	988
28. Oktober 1941	Litzmannstadt	998	13. August 1942	Theresienstadt	997
02. November 1941	Litzmannstadt	998	17. August 1942	Maly Trostinez	1003
23. November 1941	Kaunas	995	20. August 1942	Theresienstadt	997
28. November 1941	Minsk	999	27. August 1942	Theresienstadt	956
03. Dezember 1941	Riga	995	31. August 1942	Maly Trostinez	967
11. Januar 1942	Riga	1000	10. September 1942	Theresienstadt	990
26. Januar 1942	Riga	1196	14. September 1942	Maly Trostinez	992
06. Februar 1942	Riga	997	24. September 1942	Theresienstadt	1287
09. April 1942	Izbica	998	01. Oktober 1942	Theresienstadt	1290
27. April 1942	Wlodawa	998	05. Oktober 1942	Maly Trostinez	544
06. Mai 1942	Maly Trostinez	994	09. Oktober 1942	Theresienstadt	1306
12. Mai 1942	Izbica	1001			47035
15. Mai 1942	Izbica	1006			
20. Mai 1942	Maly Trostinez	986			
27. Mai 1942	Maly Trostinez	981			
02. Juni 1942	Maly Trostinez	999			

———Clara's Transport

[1] Tabelle nach Jonny Moser, "Österreich", in Wolfgang Benz (Hg.), Dimension des Völkermords. Die Zahl der jüdischen Opfer des Nationalsozialismus, München 1991, S. 22-43.

[2] List according to Jonny Moser, "Österreich", in Wolfgang Benz (ed.), Dimension des Völkermords. Die Zahl der jüdischen Opfer des Nationalsozialismus (Munich, 1991), pp. 72-43.

Source: Aspang train station – Central European Economic and Social History

Aspang train station before its destruction during World War II
Source: Aspangbahnhof - Bahnfahrt in den sicheren Tod - Wiener Zeitung
Online

L. MAIN SOURCES UTILIZED

References on the British Domestic Servant Program in England, Maly Trostinec and the Holocaust in Vienna.

Bollauf, Traude, *Dienstmädchen Emigration*, Lit. Verlag, Berlin, Germany, 2010.

Barton, Waltraud, *Ermordet in Maly Trostinec* – Conference Proceedings, New Academic Press, Vienna, Austria, 2012.

Clare, George, *Last Waltz in Vienna*, Pan Books Ltd. London, UK, 1982.

Hecht, J. Dieter, Lappin-Eppel, Elenore and Raggam-Blesch, Michaela, *Topographie der Shoah*, Mandelbaum Verlag, Vienna, Austria, 2015.

Kurzweil, Edith, *Nazi Laws and Jewish Lives*, Transaction Publishers, New Brunswick, NJ, 2004.

Offenberger, Ilana Fritz, *The Jews of Nazi Vienna*, Palgrave Macmillan, NY, NY, 2017.

Archives

Archives of the City of Vienna

Archives of the *Israelitische Kultusgemeinde*

Archives of the Joint Distribution Committee

Arsolsen Archives (Formerly ITS)

Leo Baeck Institute

National Archives of the United Kingdom

World Jewish Relief Archives

Databases

Yad Vashem Holocaust Victims Database

Documentation Center for Austrian Resistance Victims Database

United States Holocaust Memorial Museum Victims Database

Findbuch for Austrian Victims of National Socialism

Genealogy Websites

Ancestry.com

MyHeritage.com

FindMyPast.com

FamilySearch.org

Geni.org

GenTeam.eu

GesherGalicia.org

JewishGen.org

JRI-Poland.org

Libraries

National Library of Austria in Vienna

Wiener Library

Newspapers

Die Zionistische Rundschau (Vienna)

Die Neue Freie Presse (Vienna)

Vienna City Directory

Adolph Lehmann's allgemeiner Wohnungs-Anzeiger

General Websites

www.Wikipedia.org

Made in the USA
Coppell, TX
22 February 2025

46265812R00105